Washington | Adams | Jefferson | Madison
Monroe | Quincy Adams | Jackson |
Buchanan | Harrison | Tyler | Polk | Taylor
Fillmore | Pierce | van Buren | Lincoln
Johnson | Grant | Hayes | Garfield

The Presidents Speak

A COLLECTION OF SPEECHES FROM EACH OF THE PRESIDENTS OF THE UNITED STATES

Arthur | Cleveland | Harrison | McKinley | Roosevelt
Taft | Wilson | Harding | Coolidge | Hoover
Roosevelt | Truman | Eisenhower | Kennedy
Johnson | Nixon | Ford | Carter | Reagan
Bush | Clinton | G. W. Bush | Obama | Trump

The
Presidents
Speak

A COLLECTION OF SPEECHES FROM EACH
OF THE PRESIDENTS OF THE UNITED STATES

An Hachette UK Company

www.hachette.co.uk

First published in Great Britain in 2018 by Pyramid,
an imprint of Octopus Publishing Group Ltd
Carmelite House
50 Victoria Embankment
London EC4Y 0DZ
www.octopusbooks.co.uk

ISBN 978-0-7537-3320-2

A CIP catalogue record for this book is available from the British Library

Printed and bound in China

Publisher: Lucy Pessell
Editor: Sarah Vaughan
Contributing Editor: Anna Bowles
Designer: Lisa Laton
Production Controller: Katie Jervis

Note: Because they reflect the era in which they were given and the views of the people giving
them, some of the speeches in this book may contain sexist or racist terms. The publishers
apologize for any offence caused.

CONTENTS

INTRODUCTION

What is the greatest speech in American history? Opinions differ, but many would consider it to be one of those contained in this book: Abraham Lincoln's Gettysburg Address, maybe, or John F. Kennedy's Inaugural Address. Some of the greatest orators and statesmen in history have numbered among the U.S. presidents whose words are presented in these pages.

Some of these speeches mark era-defining events, such as the announcement of the withdrawal of American troops from Vietnam by Gerald Ford in April 1975, or Ronald Reagan's 1987 challenge to Soviet leader Mikhail Gorbachev to tear down the Berlin Wall. Others are more informal in tone, yet often greatly telling about the man behind the words and the challenges of the office he occupied: "If you can't stand the heat, get out of the kitchen," as Harry S. Truman summed up the job of president.

Another feature of modern oratory is that it tracks the changing face of media. Early presidents spoke to small numbers of privileged colleagues or occasional gatherings of the public who were within range of a single voice, with their words perhaps summarized in a newspaper afterwards. Now presidents use social media to address the entire world. Speeches and series like Franklin D. Roosevelt's radio-program *Fireside Chats* show how U.S. leaders experimented with and gradually harnessed the power of broadcast media to share the concerns of the nation with its people, and to woo the electorate's approval for the popularity polls. A country as great as America has always influenced the world outside its borders, and that has never been more true than today, when as the world's only Superpower the country's leader must consider the question of what is right for the billions of human beings across the world as well as the millions inside the U.S.A., and speak to them as well as his own people every time a speech is delivered or a tweet tweeted.

Among the classics here you will also find speeches from some lesser-known names. President William H. Harrison, who came to office in March 1841, had a limited chance to prove his skills as he died just a month later. Every president is represented in this book, whether by one speech or several, giving a truly comprehensive look at the oratory of the U.S. presidency as it has grown and changed with America itself since the Declaration of Independence nearly 250 years ago.

RELIGION & CULTURE

PROCLAMATION OF A DAY OF FASTING AND PRAYER

James Madison

1751–1836
4th President: March 4, 1809–March 4, 1817

Church and State are separated by the First Amendment to the Constitution, yet Christian observance has often been an important part of governance in the U.S., and before the formal establishment by Abraham Lincoln of Thanksgiving in 1863 and the annual National Day of Prayer in 1952 by Harry S. Truman, some presidents proclaimed National Days of Prayer in response to significant events. James Madison instituted two such days, including one on July 9, 1812, asking for God's intercession in the U.S.-Britain war of 1812–1815.

Whereas the Congress of the United States, by a joint resolution of the two Houses, have signified a request that a day may be recommended to be observed by the people of the United States with religious solemnity as a day of public humiliation and prayer; and whereas such a recommendation will enable the several religious denominations and societies so disposed to offer at one and the same time their common vows and adorations to Almighty God on the solemn occasion produced by the war in which He has been pleased to permit the injustice of a foreign power to involve these United States:

I do therefore recommend the third Thursday in August next as a convenient day to be set apart for the devout purposes of rendering the Sovereign of the Universe and the Benefactor of Mankind the public homage due to His holy attributes; of acknowledging the transgressions which might justly provoke the manifestations of His divine displeasure; of seeking His merciful forgiveness and His assistance in the great duties of repentance and amendment, and especially of offering fervent supplications that in the present season of calamity and war He would take the American people under His peculiar care and protection; that He would guide their public councils, animate their patriotism, and bestow His blessing on their arms; that He would inspire all nations with a love of justice and of concord and with a reverence for the unerring precept of our holy religion to do to others as they would require that others should do to them; and, finally, that, turning the hearts of our enemies from the violence and injustice which sway their councils against us, He would hasten a restoration of the blessings of peace.

"THE MAN WITH THE MUCK-RAKE" SPEECH

Theodore Roosevelt

1858–1919
26th President: September 14, 1901–March 4, 1909

"Muckraker" is now a common term for journalists who specialise in digging up scandal, and is usually pejorative in use. It refers back to a character in John Bunyan's classic Pilgrim's Progress, *who misses out on salvation because of his focus on the dirty floor, and came into its current meaning as the result of this 1906 speech by President Roosevelt. Roosevelt was conscious of the growing influence of the press, and soon after his inauguration in 1901 instigated press conferences in an attempt to manage the interface between his administration and the media. When journalists persisted in asking unwanted questions and raising awkward points, they found*

themselves criticised in turn. Many resented the term "muckraker" and regarded it as a smear designed to make their serious reporting on important issues easier to dismiss.

[…] It is very necessary that we should not flinch from seeing what is vile and debasing. There is filth on the floor, and it must be scraped up with the muck-rake; and there are times and places where this service is the most needed of all the services that can be performed. But the man who never does anything else, who never thinks or speaks or writes, save of his feats with the muck-rake, speedily becomes, not a help to society, not an incitement to good, but one of the most potent forces for evil.

[…] There are, in the body politic, economic and social, many and grave evils, and there is urgent necessity for the sternest war upon them. There should be relentless exposure of and attack upon every evil man whether politician or business man, every evil practice, whether in politics, in business, or in social life. I hail as a benefactor every writer or speaker, every man who, on the platform, or in book, magazine, or newspaper, with merciless severity makes such attack, provided always that he in his turn remembers that the attack is of use only if it is absolutely truthful. The liar is no whit better than the thief, and if his mendacity takes the form of slander, he may be worse than most thieves. It puts a premium upon knavery untruthfully to attack an honest man, or even with hysterical exaggeration to assail a bad man with untruth. An epidemic of indiscriminate assault upon character does not good, but very great harm. The soul of every scoundrel is gladdened whenever an honest man is assailed, or even when a scoundrel is untruthfully assailed.

ADDRESS TO THE AMERICAN SOCIETY OF NEWSPAPER EDITORS

Calvin Coolidge

1872–1933
30th President: August 2, 1923–March 4, 1929

This speech by Calvin Coolidge is primarily famous for the quotation "the chief business of the American people is business", but that does not do justice to its full content. Coolidge also said "the chief ideal of the American people is idealism' and laid out a vision of newspaper reporting – in those days, the only mass news media – as "an informing and enlightened epic" that when executed properly could raise rather than lower the tone of political and social debate. An ideal, perhaps, for a time when reporters were able to take a few hours to digest what they had seen rather than having to immediately write it up for their employer's website.

Newspaper men[…] endlessly discuss the question of what is news. I judge that they will go on discussing it as long as there are newspapers. It has seemed to me that quite obviously the news giving function of a newspaper cannot possibly require that it give a photographic presentation of everything that happens in the community. That is an obvious impossibility. It seems fair to say that the proper presentation of the news bears about the same relation to the whole field of happenings that a painting does to a photograph. The photograph might give the more accurate presentation of details, but in doing so it might sacrifice the opportunity the more clearly to delineate character. My college professor was wont to tell us a good many years ago that if a painting of a tree was only the exact representation of the original, so that it looked just like the tree, there would be no reason for making it; we might as well look at the tree itself. But the painting, if it is of the right sort, gives something that neither a photograph nor a view of the tree conveys. It emphasizes something of character, quality, individuality. We are not lost in looking at thorns and defects; we catch a vision of the grandeur and beauty of a king of the forest.

And so I have conceived that the news, properly presented, should be a sort of cross section of the character of current human experience. It should delineate character, quality, tendencies and implications. In this way the reporter exercises his genius. Out of the current events he does not make a drab and sordid story, but rather an informing and enlightened epic. His work becomes no longer imitative, but rises to an original art.

ADDRESS ON THE SPACE EFFORT

John F. Kennedy

1917–1963
35th President: January 20, 1961–November 22, 1963

In the early 1960s, Russia was well ahead of the U.S. in what would become known as the Space Race. President Kennedy had first announced the decision to send American astronauts to the Moon to a Joint Session of Congress in May 1961, just six weeks after cosmonaut Yuri Gagarin had become the first person to orbit the Earth beyond the planet's atmosphere. Over the program's 13 years, it is estimated to have cost anything up to $25.4 billion (in 1969 terms). It also cost the lives of three astronauts: Gus Grissom, Edward White, and Roger Chaffee were killed when Apollo 1 *exploded on its launch pad in 1967.*

President Pitzer, Mr. Vice President, Governor, Congressman Thomas, Senator Wiley, and Congressman Miller, Mr. Webb, Mr. Bell, scientists, distinguished guests, and ladies and gentlemen […]

No man can fully grasp how far and how fast we have come, but condense, if you will, the 50,000 years of man's recorded history in a time span of but a half-century.

Stated in these terms, we know very little about the first 40 years, except at the end of them advanced man had learned to use the skins of animals to cover them. Then about 10 years ago, under this standard, man emerged from his caves to construct other kinds of shelter. Only five years ago man learned to write and use a cart with wheels. Christianity began less than two years ago. The printing press came this year, and then less than two months ago, during this whole 50-year span of human history, the steam engine provided a new source of power. Newton explored the meaning of gravity. Last month electric lights and telephones and automobiles and airplanes became available. Only last week did we develop penicillin and television and nuclear power, and now if America's new spacecraft succeeds in reaching Venus, we will have literally reached the stars before midnight tonight.

This is a breathtaking pace, and such a pace cannot help but create new ills as it dispels old, new ignorance, new problems, new dangers. Surely the opening vistas of space promise high costs and hardships, as well as high reward.

So it is not surprising that some would have us stay where we are a little longer to rest, to wait. But this city of Houston, this state of Texas, this country of the United States was not built by those who waited and rested and wished to look behind them. This country was conquered by those who moved forward – and so will space […]

If this capsule history of our progress teaches us anything, it is that man, in his quest for knowledge and progress, is determined and cannot be deterred. The exploration of space will go ahead, whether we join in it or not, and it is one of the great adventures of all time, and no nation which expects to be the leader of other nations can expect to stay behind in this race for space.

Those who came before us made certain that this country rode the first waves of the industrial revolution, the first waves of modern invention, and the first wave of nuclear power, and this generation does not intend to founder in the backwash of the coming age of space. We mean to be a part of it – we mean to lead it. For the eyes of the world now look into space, to the Moon and to the planets beyond, and we have vowed that we shall not see it governed by a hostile flag of conquest, but by a banner of freedom and peace. We have vowed that we shall not see space filled with weapons of mass destruction, but with instruments of knowledge and understanding.

Yet the vows of this nation can only be fulfilled if we in this nation are first, and, therefore, we intend to be first. In short, our leadership in science and industry, our hopes for peace and security, our obligations to ourselves as well as others, all require us to make this effort, to solve these mysteries, to solve them for the good of all men, and to become the world's leading space-faring nation.

We set sail on this new sea because there is new knowledge to be gained, and new rights to be won, and they must be won and used for the progress of all people.

For space science, like nuclear science and all technology, has no conscience of its own. Whether it will become a force for good or ill depends on man, and only if the United States occupies a position of pre-eminence can we help decide whether this new ocean will be a sea of peace or a new terrifying theater of war. I do not say that we should or will go unprotected against the hostile misuse of space any more than we go unprotected against the hostile use of land or sea, but I do say that space can be explored and mastered without feeding the fires of war, without repeating the mistakes that man has made in extending his writ around this globe of ours [...]

We choose to go to the Moon. We choose to go to the Moon in this decade and do the other things, not because they are easy, but because they are hard, because that goal will serve to organize and measure the best of our energies and skills, because that challenge is one that we are willing to accept, one we are unwilling to postpone, and one which we intend to win, and the others, too [...]

In the last 24 hours, we have seen facilities now being created for the greatest and most complex exploration in man's history. We have felt the ground shake and the air shattered by the testing of a Saturn C-1 booster rocket, many times as powerful as the Atlas which launched John Glenn, generating power equivalent to 10,000 automobiles with their accelerators on the floor. We have seen the site where five F-1 rocket engines, each one as powerful as all eight engines of the Saturn combined, will be clustered together to make the advanced Saturn missile, assembled in a new building to be built at Cape Canaveral as tall as a 48-story structure, as wide as a city block, and as long as two lengths of this field.

Within these last 19 months at least 45 satellites have circled the Earth. Some 40 of them were made in the United States of America and they were far more sophisticated and supplied far more knowledge to the people of the world than those of the Soviet Union.

The Mariner spacecraft now on its way to Venus is the most intricate instrument in the history of space science. The accuracy of that shot is comparable to firing a missile from Cape Canaveral and dropping it in this stadium between the 40-yard lines.

Transit satellites are helping our ships at sea to steer a safer course. Tiros satellites have given us unprecedented warnings of hurricanes and storms, and will do the same for forest fires and icebergs [...] To be sure, all this costs us all a good deal of money. This year's space budget is three times what it was in January 1961, and it is greater than the space budget of the previous eight years combined. That budget now stands at $5,400 million a year – a staggering sum, though somewhat less than we pay for cigarettes and cigars every year. Space expenditures will soon rise some more, from 40 cents per person per week to more than 50 cents a week for every man, woman and child in the United States, for we have given this program a high national priority – even though I realize that this is in some measure an act of faith and vision, for we do not now know what benefits await us. But if I were to say, my fellow citizens, that we shall send to the Moon, 240,000 miles away from the control station in Houston, a giant rocket more than 300 feet tall, the length of this football field, made of new metal alloys, some of which have not yet been invented, capable of standing heat and stresses several times more than have ever been experienced, fitted together with a precision better than the finest watch, carrying all the equipment needed for propulsion, guidance, control, communications, food and survival, on an untried mission, to an unknown celestial body, and then return it safely to Earth, re-entering the atmosphere at speeds of over 25,000 miles per hour, causing heat about half that of the temperature of the Sun – almost as hot as it is here today – and do all this, and do it right, and do it first before this decade is out – then we must be bold [...]

And I am delighted that this university is playing a part in putting a man on the Moon as part of a great national effort of the United States of America. Many years ago the great British explorer George Mallory, who was to die on Mount Everest, was asked why did he want to climb it. He said, "Because it is there."

Well, space is there, and we're going to climb it, and the Moon and the planets are there, and new hopes for knowledge and peace are there. And, therefore, as we set sail we ask God's blessing on the most hazardous and dangerous and greatest adventure on which man has ever embarked.

CHALLENGER SPEECH

Ronald Reagan

1911–2004
40th President: January 20, 1981–January 20, 1989

Just 73 seconds after lift-off into mission STS-51-L, the Space Shuttle Challenger *disintegrated in a ball of flame, resulting in the loss of the seven astronauts – including high-school teacher Christa McAuliffe. That evening, instead of the State of the Union address he had been scheduled to give, the President paid tribute to them. After fragments of the Shuttle and the external boosters and fuel tank were collected, a piece-by-piece investigation concluded that an O-ring seal in one of the boosters had failed, which led to a fireball and the disintegration of the spacecraft. The crew compartment was found in the Gulf of Mexico.*

Ladies and gentlemen, I'd planned to speak to you tonight to report on the state of the Union, but the events of earlier today have led me to change those plans. Today is a day for mourning and remembering. Nancy and I are pained to the core by the tragedy of the Shuttle *Challenger*. We know we share this pain with all of the people of our country. This is truly a national loss.

Nineteen years ago, almost to the day, we lost three astronauts in a terrible accident on the ground. But we've never lost an astronaut in flight; we've never had a tragedy like this. And perhaps we've forgotten the courage it took for the crew of the shuttle. But they, the *Challenger* Seven, were aware of the dangers, but overcame them and did their jobs brilliantly. We mourn seven heroes: Michael Smith, Dick Scobee, Judith Resnik, Ronald McNair, Ellison Onizuka, Gregory Jarvis, and Christa McAuliffe. We mourn their loss as a nation together […]

I've always had great faith in and respect for our space program, and what happened today does nothing to diminish it. We don't hide our space program. We don't keep secrets and cover things up. We do it all up front and in public. That's the way freedom is, and we wouldn't change it for a minute. We'll continue our quest in space. There will be more Shuttle flights and more shuttle crews and, yes, more volunteers, more civilians, more teachers in space. Nothing ends here; our hopes and our journeys continue. I want to add that I wish I could talk to every man and woman who works for NASA or who worked on this mission and tell them: "Your dedication and professionalism have moved and impressed us for decades. And we know of your anguish. We share it." […]

The crew of the Space Shuttle *Challenger* honored us by the manner in which they lived their lives. We will never forget them, nor the last time we saw them, this morning, as they prepared for their journey and waved goodbye and "slipped the surly bonds of earth" to "touch the face of God."

HUMANITY & LIBERTY

THE DECLARATION OF INDEPENDENCE

Thomas Jefferson

1743–1826
3rd President: March 4, 1801–March 4, 1809

One year into the American Revolutionary War, delegates to the Second Continental Congress voted on July 2, 1776 to declare independence from the British Crown. Two days later, the text – designed to explain to the population why Congress had voted for independence – was finalized then printed and distributed. In the preceding decade, the British Crown had increased taxation on its colonies to pay off its vast national debt and laws had been passed by the British Parliament to increase its control over the colonies, leading some to question whether it had violated the latter's rights and therefore its own right to rule.

When, in the course of human events, it becomes necessary for one people to dissolve the political bonds which have connected them with another, and to assume among the powers of the earth, the separate and equal station to which the laws of nature and of nature's God entitle them, a decent respect to the opinions of mankind requires that they should declare the causes which impel them to the separation.

   We hold these truths to be self-evident, that all men are created equal, that they are endowed by their Creator with certain unalienable rights, that among these are life, liberty and the pursuit of happiness. That to secure these rights, governments are instituted among men, deriving their just powers from the consent of the governed. That whenever any form of government becomes destructive to these ends, it is the right of the people to alter or to abolish it, and to institute new government, laying its foundation on such principles and organizing its powers in such form, as to them shall seem most likely to effect their safety and happiness. Prudence, indeed, will dictate that governments long established should not be changed for light and transient causes; and accordingly all experience hath shown that mankind are more disposed to suffer, while evils are sufferable, than to right themselves by abolishing the forms to which they are accustomed. But when a long train of abuses and usurpations, pursuing invariably the same object evinces a design to reduce them under absolute despotism, it is their right, it is their duty, to throw off such government, and to provide new guards for their future security. Such has been the patient sufferance of these colonies; and such is now the necessity which constrains them to alter their former systems of government. The history of the present King of Great Britain is a history of repeated injuries and usurpations, all having in direct object the establishment of an absolute tyranny over these states. To prove this, let facts be submitted to a candid world.

He has refused his assent to laws, the most wholesome and necessary for the public good.

He has forbidden his governors to pass laws of immediate and pressing importance, unless suspended in their operation till his assent should be obtained; and when so suspended, he has utterly neglected to attend to them.

He has refused to pass other laws for the accommodation of large districts of people, unless those people would relinquish the right of representation in the legislature, a right inestimable to them and formidable to tyrants only.

He has called together legislative bodies at places unusual, uncomfortable, and distant from the depository of their public records, for the sole purpose of fatiguing them into compliance with his measures.

He has dissolved representative houses repeatedly, for opposing with manly firmness his invasions on the rights of the people.

He has refused for a long time, after such dissolutions, to cause others to be elected; whereby the legislative powers, incapable of annihilation, have returned to the people at large for their exercise; the state remaining in the meantime exposed to all the dangers of invasion from without, and convulsions within.

He has endeavored to prevent the population of these states; for that purpose obstructing the laws for naturalization of foreigners; refusing to pass others to encourage their migration hither, and raising the conditions of new appropriations of lands.

He has obstructed the administration of justice, by refusing his assent to laws for establishing judiciary powers.

He has made judges dependent on his will alone, for the tenure of their offices, and the amount and payment of their salaries.

He has erected a multitude of new offices, and sent hither swarms of officers to harass our people, and eat out their substance.

He has kept among us, in times of peace, standing armies without the consent of our legislature.

He has affected to render the military independent of and superior to civil power.

He has combined with others to subject us to a jurisdiction foreign to our constitution, and unacknowledged by our laws; giving his assent to their acts of pretended legislation:

For quartering large bodies of armed troops among us;

For protecting them, by mock trial, from punishment for any murders which they should commit on the inhabitants of these states;

For cutting off our trade with all parts of the world;

For imposing taxes on us without our consent;

For depriving us in many cases, of the benefits of trial by jury;

For transporting us beyond seas to be tried for pretended offenses;

For abolishing the free system of English laws in a neighbouring province, establishing therein an arbitrary government, and enlarging its boundaries so as to render it at once an example and fit instrument for introducing the same absolute rule in these colonies;

For taking away our charters, abolishing our most valuable laws, and altering fundamentally the forms of our governments;

For suspending our own legislatures, and declaring themselves invested with power to legislate for us in all cases whatsoever.

He has abdicated government here, by declaring us out of his protection and waging war against us.

He has plundered our seas, ravaged our coasts, burned our towns, and destroyed the lives of our people.

He is at this time transporting large armies of foreign mercenaries to complete the works of death, desolation and tyranny, already begun with circumstances of cruelty and perfidy scarcely paralleled in the most barbarous ages, and totally unworthy the head of a civilized nation.

He has constrained our fellow citizens taken captive on the high seas to bear arms against their country, to become the executioners of their friends and brethren, or to fall themselves by their hands.

He has excited domestic insurrections amongst us, and has endeavored to bring on the inhabitants of our frontiers, the merciless Indian savages, whose known rule of warfare, is undistinguished destruction of all ages, sexes, and conditions.

In every stage of these oppressions we have petitioned for redress in the most humble terms: our repeated petitions have been answered only by repeated injury.

A prince, whose character is thus marked by every act which may define a tyrant, is unfit to be the ruler of a free people.

Nor have we been wanting in attention to our British brethren. We have warned them from time to time of attempts by their legislature to extend an unwarrantable jurisdiction over us. We have reminded them of the circumstances of our emigration and settlement here. We have appealed to their native justice and magnanimity, and we have conjured them by the ties of our common kindred to disavow these usurpations, which, would inevitably interrupt our connections and correspondence.

They too have been deaf to the voice of justice and of consanguinity. We must, therefore, acquiesce in the necessity, which denounces our separation, and hold them, as we hold the rest of mankind, enemies in war, in peace friends.

We, therefore, the representatives of the United States of America, in General Congress, assembled, appealing to the Supreme Judge of the world for the rectitude of our intentions, do, in the name, and by the authority of the good people of these colonies, solemnly publish and declare, that these united colonies are, and of right ought to be free and independent states; that they are absolved from all allegiance to the British Crown, and that all political connection between them and the state of Great Britain, is and ought to be totally dissolved; and that as free and independent states, they have full power to levy war, conclude peace, contract alliances, establish commerce, and to do all other acts and things which independent states may of right do. And for the support of this declaration, with a firm reliance on the protection of Divine Providence, we mutually pledge to each other our lives, our fortunes and our sacred honor.

LETTER TO AN IRISH IMMIGRANT

George Washington

1732–1799
1st President: April 30, 1789–March 4, 1797

Less than three months after the signature of the treaty that ended the Revolutionary Wars, George Washington addressed a group of Irish immigrants who had recently arrived in New York. For the next few years, he retired to his plantation at Mount Vernon. He re-entered politics in 1787, to preside over the Philadelpia Convention that drafted the Constitution of the United States of America and become the first President of the U.S.A. in 1789. In fact, immigration did not increase markedly until the 1830s, but from then on it grew rapidly. Irish people, especially, came to work in the industries that were springing up in American cities.

Gentlemen: The testimony of your satisfaction at the glorious termination of the late contest, and your indulgent opinion of my Agency in it, affords me singular pleasure and merits my warmest acknowledgment.

If the Example of the Americans successfully contending in the Cause of Freedom, can be of any use to other Nations; we shall have an additional Motive for rejoycing at so prosperous an Event. It was not an uninteresting consideration to learn that the Kingdom of Ireland, by a bold and manly conduct, had obtained the redress of many of its grievances; and it is much to be wished that the blessings of equal Liberty and unrestrained Commerce may yet prevail more extensively; in the mean time, you may be assured, Gentlemen, that the Hospitality and Beneficence of your Countrymen, to our Brethren who have been Prisoners of War, are neither unknown, or unregarded.

The bosom of America is open to receive not only the Opulent and respectable Stranger, but the oppressed and persecuted of all Nations And Religions; whom we shall welcome to a participation of all our rights and privileges, if by decency and propriety of conduct they appear to merit the enjoyment.

INDEPENDENCE DAY SPEECH

John Quincy Adams

1767–1848
6th President: March 4, 1825–March 4, 1829

John Quincy Adams' famous Independence Day speech of 1821 struck the notes of American pride and independence that had by then become familiar, and remain so now. However, beyond the high principles, this particular speech became the basis for the Monroe Doctrine of opposing European intervention in the Americas (see page 137). In other words, if the old powers would keep their fingers out of the United States' business, it would oblige them in return.

Wherever the standard of freedom and independence has been or shall be unfurled, there will her heart, her benedictions and her prayers be. But she goes not abroad in search of monsters to destroy. She is the well-wisher to the freedom and independence of all. She is the champion and vindicator only of her own. She will recommend the general cause, by the countenance of her voice, and the benignant sympathy of her example.

ADDRESS TO THE CREEK
NATIONAL COUNCIL

Andrew Jackson

1767–1845
7th President: March 4, 1829–March 4, 1837

The paternalistic, patronizing tone in which President Jackson addressed the people of the Creek nation – some of whom had been his allies in the Creek War of 1813–1814 – is astonishing. Within little more than a year, the Indian Removal Act had been passed and then enforced, often violently, and movement of Native Americans westwards had begun. The Creek had already given up 23,000,000 acres of land (in Alabama and Georgia) to the settlers in the Treaty of Fort Jackson of 1814.

You and my white children are too near to each other to live in harmony and peace […] Beyond the great River Mississippi […] your father has provided a country large enough for all of you, and he advises you to remove to it. There your white brothers will not trouble you; they will have no claim to the land […] It will be yours forever.

PROCLAMATION REGARDING NULLIFICATION

Andrew Jackson

1767–1845
7th President: March 4, 1829–March 4, 1837

In 1828, the Adams government had introduced a tariff on imported goods (known by its detractors as the Tariff of Abominations), which affected states of the Deep South far more than the industrializing states of the North. Because the South imported more goods from Europe and because of the decline in trade, their traditional customers no longer had the money to pay for the South's main crops such as cotton. In 1832, the South Carolina legislature passed several laws seeking to nullify Federal law and threatening secession. Although President Jackson sympathized to some extent, he was not going to allow states to overturn Federal laws that did not suit them, so he threatened to send in a military force.

[...] Whereas the said ordinance prescribes to the people of South Carolina a course of conduct in direct violation of their duty as citizens of the United States, contrary to the laws of their country, subversive of its Constitution, and having for its object the instruction of the Union – that Union, which, coeval with our political existence, led our fathers, without any other ties to unite them than those of patriotism and common cause, through the sanguinary struggle to a glorious independence – that sacred Union, hitherto inviolate, which, perfected by our happy Constitution, has brought us, by the favor of Heaven, to a state of prosperity at home and high consideration abroad, rarely, if ever, equaled in the history of nations; to preserve this bond of our political existence from destruction, to maintain inviolate this state of national honor and prosperity, and to justify the confidence my fellow-citizens have reposed in me, I, Andrew Jackson, President of the United States, have thought proper to issue this my PROCLAMATION, stating my views of the Constitution and laws applicable to the measures adopted by the Convention of South Carolina, and to the reasons they have put forth to sustain them, declaring the course which duty will require me to pursue, and, appealing to the understanding and patriotism of the people, warn them of the consequences that must inevitably result from an observance of the dictates of the Convention [...]

The ordinance is founded, not on the indefeasible right of resisting acts which are plainly unconstitutional, and too oppressive to be endured, but on the strange position that any one State may not only declare an act of Congress void, but prohibit its execution – that they may do this consistently with the Constitution – that the true construction of that instrument permits a State to retain its place in the Union, and yet be bound by no other of its laws than those it may choose to consider as constitutional. It is true they add, that to justify this abrogation of a law, it must be palpably contrary to the Constitution, but it is evident, that to give the right of resisting laws of that description, coupled with the uncontrolled right to decide what laws deserve that character, is to give the power of resisting all laws.

For, as by the theory, there is no appeal, the reasons alleged by the State, good or bad, must prevail. If it should be said that public opinion is a sufficient check against the abuse of this power, it may be asked why it is not deemed a sufficient guard against the passage of an unconstitutional act by Congress [...] But reasoning on this subject is superfluous, when our social compact in express terms declares, that the laws of the United States, its Constitution, and treaties made under it, are the supreme law of the land; and for greater caution adds, "that the judges in every State shall be bound thereby, anything in the Constitution or laws of any State to the contrary notwithstanding." And it may be asserted, without fear of refutation, that no federative government could exist without a similar provision. Look, for a moment, to the consequence. If South Carolina considers the revenue laws unconstitutional, and has a right to prevent their execution in the port of Charleston, there would be a clear constitutional objection to their collection in every other port, and no revenue could be collected anywhere; for all imposts must be equal. It is no answer to repeat that an unconstitutional law is no law, so long as the question of its legality is to be decided by the State itself, for every law operating injuriously upon any local interest will be perhaps thought, and certainly represented, as unconstitutional, and, as has been shown, there is no appeal [...]

The most important among these objects [in the ordinance], that which is placed first in rank, on which all the others rest, is "to form a more perfect Union." Now, is it possible that, even if there were no express provision giving supremacy to the Constitution and laws of the United States over those of the States, it can be conceived that an Instrument made for the purpose of "forming a more perfect Union" than that of the confederation, could be so constructed by the assembled wisdom of our country as to substitute for that confederation a form of government, dependent for its existence on the local interest, the party spirit of a State, or of a prevailing faction in a State? [...]

Here is a law of the United States, not even pretended to be unconstitutional, repealed by the authority of a small majority of the voters of a single State. Here is a provision of the Constitution which is solemnly abrogated by the same authority.

On such expositions and reasonings, the ordinance grounds not only an assertion of the right to annul the laws of which it complains, but to enforce it by a threat of seceding from the Union if any attempt is made to execute them.

This right to secede is deduced [in the ordinance] from the nature of the Constitution, which they say is a compact between sovereign States who have preserved their whole sovereignty, and therefore are subject to no superior; that because they made the compact, they can break it when in their opinion it has been departed from by the other States. Fallacious as this course of reasoning is, it enlists State pride, and finds advocates in the honest prejudices of those who have not studied the nature of our government sufficiently to see the radical error on which it rests.

The people of the United States formed the Constitution, acting through the State legislatures, in making the compact, to meet and discuss its provisions, and acting in separate conventions when they ratified those provisions; but the terms used in its construction show it to be a government in which the people of all the States collectively are represented. We are ONE PEOPLE in the choice of the President and Vice President. Here the States have no other agency than to direct the mode in which the vote shall be given. The candidates having the majority of all the votes are chosen. The electors of a majority of States may have given their votes for one candidate, and yet another may be chosen. The people, then, and not the States, are represented in the executive branch [...]

The Constitution of the United States, then, forms a government, not a league, and whether it be formed by compact between the States, or in any other manner, its character is the same. It is a government in which all the people are represented, which operates directly on the people individually, not upon the States; they retained all the power they did not grant. But each State having expressly parted with so many powers as to constitute jointly with the other States a single nation, cannot from that period possess any right to secede, because such secession does not break a league, but destroys the unity of a nation, and any injury to that unity is not only a breach which would result from the contravention of a compact, but it is an offense against the whole Union [...]

Because the Union was formed by compact, it is said [in the Ordinance] the parties to that compact may, when they feel themselves aggrieved, depart from it; but it is precisely because it is a compact that they cannot [...] An attempt by force of arms to destroy a government is an offense, by whatever means the constitutional compact may have been formed; and such government has the right, by the law of self-defense, to pass acts for punishing the offender, unless that right is modified, restrained, or resumed by the constitutional act. In our system, although it is modified in the case of treason, yet authority is expressly given to pass all laws necessary to carry its powers into effect, and under this grant provision has been made for punishing acts which obstruct the due administration of the laws [...]

The States severally have not retained their entire sovereignty. It has been shown that in becoming parts of a nation, not members of a league, they surrendered many of their essential parts of sovereignty. The right to make treaties, declare war, levy taxes, exercise exclusive judicial and legislative powers, were all functions of sovereign power. The States, then, for all these important purposes, were no longer sovereign. The allegiance of their citizens was transferred in the first instance to the government of the United States; they became American citizens, and owed obedience to the Constitution of the United States, and to laws made in conformity with the powers vested in Congress. This last position has not been, and cannot be, denied. How then, can that State be said to be sovereign and independent whose citizens owe obedience to laws not made by it, and whose magistrates are sworn to disregard those laws, when they come in conflict with those passed by another? [...]

This, then, is the position in which we stand. A small majority of the citizens of one State in the Union have elected delegates to a State convention; that convention has ordained that all the revenue laws of the United States must be repealed, or that they are no longer a member of the Union. The governor of that State has recommended to the legislature the raising of an army to carry the secession into effect, and that he may be empowered to give clearances to vessels in the name of the State [...]

Fellow-citizens! the momentous case is before you. On your undivided support of your government depends the decision of the great question it involves, whether your sacred Union will be preserved, and the blessing it secures to us as one people shall be perpetuated. No one can doubt that the unanimity with which that decision will be expressed, will he such as to inspire new confidence in republican institutions, and that the prudence, the wisdom, and the courage which it will bring to their defense, will transmit them unimpaired and invigorated to our children.

May the Great Ruler of nations grant that the signal blessings with which he has favored ours may not, by the madness of party or personal ambition, be disregarded and lost, and may His wise providence bring those who have produced this crisis to see the folly, before they feel the misery, of civil strife, and inspire a returning veneration for that Union which, if we may dare to penetrate his designs, he has chosen, as the only means of attaining the high destinies to which we may reasonably aspire.

PEORIA SPEECH

Abraham Lincoln

1809–1865
16th President: 4 March 1861–15 April 1865

Although Abraham Lincoln and Judge Stephen Douglas – the author of the Kansas–Nebraska Act – most famously clashed during their debates leading up to the elections for the Senate in 1858, they had also argued during the campaign in 1854. In the speech he gave at Peoria, Illinois, in October 1858, Lincoln answered Douglas' three-hour speech with one of his own – equally long – the most important points of which are below.

The repeal of the Missouri Compromise, and the propriety of its restoration, constitute the subject of what I am about to say [...]

[...] With the author of the Declaration of Independence, the policy of prohibiting slavery in new territory originated. Thus, away back of the constitution, in the pure fresh, free breath of the revolution, the State of Virginia, and the National Congress put that policy in practice. Thus through 60-odd of the best years of the republic did that policy steadily work to its great and beneficent end. And thus, in those five states, and five millions of free, enterprising people, we have before us the rich fruits of this policy. But now new light breaks upon us. Now Congress declares this ought never to have been; and the like of it, must never be again. The sacred right of self government is grossly violated by it! We even find some men, who drew their first breath, and every other breath of their lives, under this very restriction, now live in dread of absolute suffocation, if they should be restricted in the "sacred right' of taking slaves to Nebraska. That perfect liberty they sigh for – the liberty of making slaves of other people – Jefferson never thought of; their own father never thought of; they never thought of themselves, a year ago. How fortunate for them, they did not sooner become sensible of their great misery! Oh, how difficult it is to treat with respect, such assaults upon all we have ever really held sacred […]

I think, and shall try to show, that it is wrong; wrong in its direct effect, letting slavery into Kansas and Nebraska – and wrong in its prospective principle, allowing it to spread to every other part of the wide world, where men can be found inclined to take it.

This declared indifference, but as I must think, covert real zeal for the spread of slavery, I can not but hate. I hate it because of the monstrous injustice of slavery itself. I hate it because it deprives our republican example of its just influence in the world – enables the enemies of free institutions, with plausibility, to taunt us as hypocrites – causes the real friends of freedom to doubt our sincerity, and especially because it forces so many really good men amongst ourselves into an open war with the very fundamental principles of civil liberty – criticizing the Declaration of Independence, and insisting that there is no right principle of action but self-interest […]

[…] Equal justice to the south, it is said, requires us to consent to the extending of slavery to new countries. That is to say, inasmuch as you do not object to my taking my hog to Nebraska, therefore I must not object to you taking your slave. Now, I admit this is perfectly logical, if there is no difference between hogs and Negroes. But while you thus require me to deny the humanity of the Negro, I wish to ask whether you of the south yourselves, have ever been willing to do as much? […]In 1820, you joined the north, almost unanimously, in declaring the African slave trade piracy, and in annexing to it the punishment of death. Why did you do this? If you did not feel that it was wrong, why did you join in providing that men should be hung for it? The practice was no more than bringing wild Negroes from Africa, to sell to such as would buy them. But you never thought of hanging men for catching and selling wild horses, wild buffaloes or wild bears [...]

And now, why will you ask us to deny the humanity of the slave and estimate him only as the equal of the hog? Why ask us to do what you will not do yourselves? Why ask us to do for nothing, what two hundred million of dollars could not induce you to do?

But one great argument in the support of the repeal of the Missouri Compromise, is still to come. That argument is "the sacred right of self government." It seems our distinguished Senator has found great difficulty in getting his antagonists, even in the Senate to meet him fairly on this argument [...]

I trust I understand, and truly estimate the right of self-government. My faith in the proposition that each man should do precisely as he pleases with all which is exclusively his own, lies at the foundation of the sense of justice there is in me. I extend the principles to communities of men, as well as to individuals. I so extend it, because it is politically wise, as well as naturally just; politically wise, in saving us from broils about matters which do not concern us. Here, or at Washington, I would not trouble myself with the oyster laws of Virginia, or the cranberry laws of Indiana.

The doctrine of self-government is right – absolutely and eternally right – but it has no just application, as here attempted. Or perhaps I should rather say that whether it has such just application depends upon whether a Negro is not or is a man. If he is not a man, why in that case, he who is a man may, as a matter of self-government, do just as he pleases with him. But if the Negro is a man, is it not to that extent, a total destruction of self-government, to say that he too shall not govern himself? When the white man governs himself that is self-government; but when he governs himself, and also governs another man, that is more than self-government – that is despotism. If the Negro is a man, why then my ancient faith teaches me that "all men are created equal;" and that there can be no moral right in connection with one man's making a slave of another.

Judge Douglas frequently, with bitter irony and sarcasm, paraphrases our argument by saying "The white people of Nebraska are good enough to govern themselves, but they are not good enough to govern a few miserable Negroes!" Well I doubt not that the people of Nebraska are, and will continue to be as good as the average of people elsewhere. I do not say the contrary. What I do say is, that no man is good enough to govern another man, without that other's consent. I say this is the leading principle – the sheet anchor of American republicanism. Our Declaration of Independence says:

"We hold these truths to be self evident: that all men are created equal; that they are endowed by their Creator with certain inalienable rights; that among these are life, liberty and the pursuit of happiness. That to secure these rights, governments are instituted among men, deriving their just powers from the consent of the governed." [...]

[...] I particularly object to the new position which the avowed principle of this Nebraska law gives to slavery in the body politic. I object to it because it assumes that there can be moral right in the enslaving of one man by another. I object to it as a dangerous dalliance for a few [free?] people – a sad evidence that, feeling prosperity we forget right – that liberty, as a principle, we have ceased to revere. I object to it because the fathers of the republic eschewed, and rejected it. The argument of "Necessity" was the only argument they ever admitted in favor of slavery; and so far, and so far only as it carried them, did they ever go. They found the institution existing among us, which they could not help; and they cast blame upon the British King for having permitted its introduction. before the constitution, they prohibited its introduction into the northwestern Territory – the only country we owned, then free from it. at the framing and adoption of the constitution, they forbore to so much as mention the word "slave" or "slavery" in the whole instrument. In the provision for the recovery of fugitives, the slave is spoken of as a "person held to service or labor." In that prohibiting the abolition of the African slave trade for 20 years, that trade is spoken of as "The migration or importation of such persons as any of the States now existing, shall think proper to admit," &c. These are the only provisions alluding to slavery. Thus, the thing is hid away, in the constitution, just as an afflicted man hides away a wen or a cancer, which he dares not cut out at once, lest he bleed to death; with the promise, nevertheless, that the cutting may begin at the end of a given time. Less than this our fathers could not do; and now [more?] they would not do. Necessity drove them so far, and farther, they would not go. But this is not all. The earliest Congress, under the constitution, took the same view of slavery. They hedged and hemmed it in to the narrowest limits of necessity.

In 1794, they prohibited an out-going slave-trade – that is, the taking of slaves from the United States to sell.

In 1798, they prohibited the bringing of slaves from Africa, into the Mississippi Territory – this territory then comprising what are now the States of Mississippi and Alabama. This was ten years before they had the authority to do the same thing as to the States existing at the adoption of the constitution.

In 1800, they prohibited American citizens from trading in slaves between foreign countries – as, for instance, from Africa to Brazil.

In 1803, they passed a law in aid of one or two State laws, in restraint of the internal slave trade. In 1807, in apparent hot haste, they passed the law, nearly a year in advance to take effect the first day of 1808 – the very first day the constitution would permit – prohibiting the African slave trade by heavy pecuniary and corporal penalties.

In 1820, finding these provisions ineffectual, they declared the trade piracy, and annexed to it, the extreme penalty of death. While all this was passing in the general government, five or six of the original slave States had adopted systems of gradual emancipation; and by which the institution was rapidly becoming extinct within these limits […]

But now it is to be transformed into a "sacred right." Nebraska brings it forth, places it on the high road to extension and perpetuity; and, with a pat on its back, says to it, "Go, and God speed you." Henceforth it is to be the chief jewel of the nation – the very figure-head of the ship of State. Little by little, but steadily as man's march to the grave, we have been giving up the old for the new faith. Near 80 years ago we began by declaring that all men are created equal; but now from that beginning we have run down to the other declaration, that for some men to enslave others is a "sacred right of self-government." These principles cannot stand together. They are as opposite as God and Mammon; and whoever holds to the one, must despise the other. When Pettit, in connection with his support of the Nebraska bill, called the Declaration of Independence "a self-evident lie" he only did what consistency and candor require all other Nebraska men to do. Of the 40-odd Nebraska Senators who sat present and heard him, no one rebuked him. Nor am I apprized that any Nebraska newspaper, or any Nebraska orator, in the whole nation, has ever yet rebuked him […]

Our republican robe is soiled, and trailed in the dust. Let us repurify it. Let us turn and wash it white, in the spirit, if not the blood, of the Revolution. Let us turn slavery from its claims of "moral right," back upon its existing legal rights, and its arguments of "necessity." Let us return it to the position our fathers gave it; and there let it rest in peace. Let us re-adopt the Declaration of Independence, and with it, the practices, and policy, which harmonize with it. Let north and south – let all Americans – let all lovers of liberty everywhere – join in the great and good work. If we do this, we shall not only have saved the Union; but we shall have so saved it, as to make, and to keep it, forever worthy of the saving. We shall have so saved it, that the succeeding millions of free happy people, the world over, shall rise up, and call us blessed […]

SENATORIAL CAMPAIGN MEETING SPEECH

Abraham Lincoln

1809–1865
16th President: 4 March 1861–15 April 1865

Abraham Lincoln is supposed to have said this at a Senatorial campaign meeting in Clinton, Illinois, but this has never been proved and it is not in his published works. What is known about the speech he made on September 8 is that he spent a part of it refuting an attack by his Democrat rival for the Senate seat, Judge Stephen Douglas, to the effect that a speech he had given in Springfield, Illinois, earlier in the campaign made it clear that he was in favour of giving equal rights to slaves. Douglas had been instrumental in the Kansas–Nebraska Act, which sought to give new territories the right to decide on whether to allow slavery, which ran against earlier Federal legislation. The opposition movement against this Act became the Republican Party.

If you once forfeit the confidence of your fellow citizens, you can never regain their respect and esteem. You may fool all the people some of the time; you can even fool some of the people all the time; but you can't fool all of the people all of the time.

EMANCIPATION PROCLAMATION

Abraham Lincoln

1809–1865

16th President: 4 March 1861–15 April 1865

In his second State of the Union Address, in December 1862, Lincoln referred to the draft Emancipation Proclamation and justified it to a partially hostile Congress: "In giving freedom to the slave, we assure freedom to the free – honorable alike in what we give and what we preserve. We shall nobly save or meanly lose the last, best hope of earth." The aim mentioned in the Proclamation of setting up colonies for freed slaves never came to fruition. The move to link the end of slavery with the future of the Union was a key strategy toward the end of the war. Lincoln had written to the New York Tribune *in 1862, saying that if he could preserve the Union without ending slavery he would, but that it was not possible. The proclamation read as follow:*

Whereas on the 22nd day of September, A.D. 1862, a proclamation was issued by the President of the United States, containing, among other things, the following, to wit:

That on the 1st day of January, A.D. 1863, all persons held as slaves within any State or designated part of a State the people whereof shall then be in rebellion against the United States shall be then, thenceforward, and forever free; and the executive government of the United States, including the military and naval authority thereof, will recognize and maintain the freedom of such persons and will do no act or acts to repress such persons, or any of them, in any efforts they may make for their actual freedom.

That the executive will on the 1st day of January aforesaid, by proclamation, designate the States and parts of States, if any, in which the people thereof, respectively, shall then be in rebellion against the United States; and the fact that any State or the people thereof shall on that day be in good faith represented in the Congress of the United States by members chosen thereto at elections wherein a majority of the qualified voters of such States shall have participated shall, in the absence of strong countervailing testimony, be deemed conclusive evidence that such State and the people thereof are not then in rebellion against the United States. Now, therefore, I, Abraham Lincoln, President of the United States, by virtue of the power in me vested as Commander-In-Chief of the Army and Navy of the United States in time of actual armed rebellion against the authority and government of the United States, and as a fit and necessary war measure for suppressing said rebellion, do, on this 1st day of January, A.D. 1863, and in accordance with my purpose so to do, publicly proclaimed for the full period of 100 days from the first day above mentioned, order and designate as the States and parts of States wherein the people thereof, respectively, are this day in rebellion against the United States the following, to wit:

Arkansas, Texas, Louisiana (except the parishes of St. Bernard, Plaquemines, Jefferson, St. John, St. Charles, St. James, Ascension, Assumption, Terrebone, Lafourche, St. Mary, St. Martin, and Orleans, including the city of New Orleans), Mississippi, Alabama, Florida, Georgia, South Carolina, North Carolina, and Virginia (except the 48 counties designated as West Virginia, and also the counties of Berkeley, Accomac, Northhampton, Elizabeth City, York, Princess Anne, and Norfolk, including the cities of Norfolk and Portsmouth), and which excepted parts are for the present left precisely as if this proclamation were not issued.

And by virtue of the power and for the purpose aforesaid, I do order and declare that all persons held as slaves within said designated States and parts of States are, and henceforward shall be, free; and that the Executive Government of the United States, including the military and naval authorities thereof, will recognize and maintain the freedom of said persons.

And I hereby enjoin upon the people so declared to be free to abstain from all violence, unless in necessary self-defense; and I recommend to them that, in all case when allowed, they labor faithfully for reasonable wages.

And I further declare and make known that such persons of suitable condition will be received into the armed service of the United States to garrison forts, positions, stations, and other places, and to man vessels of all sorts in said service.

And upon this act, sincerely believed to be an act of justice, warranted by the Constitution upon military necessity, I invoke the considerate judgment of mankind and the gracious favor of Almighty God.

ADDRESS ON CIVIL RIGHTS

John F. Kennedy

1917–1963
35th President: January 20, 1961–November 22, 1963

On the day that he had sent the Alabama National Guard to the University of Alabama to ensure that two African-American students would gain access to their classes in the face of opposition from Governor Wallace, President Kennedy addressed the nation from the Oval Office. Having initially been wary of alienating southern Democrats he decided, in the summer of 1963, to start enacting legislation enshrining the right to an equal education, to a vote, to equal treatment in shops and restaurants, etc. The scale of the task was made all too apparent the following day when a Mississippi civil-rights activist, Medgar Evers, was murdered by the Ku Klux Klan.

This afternoon, following a series of threats and defiant statements, the presence of Alabama National Guardsmen was required on the University of Alabama to carry out the final and unequivocal order of the United States District Court of the Northern District of Alabama. That order called for the admission of two clearly qualified young Alabama residents who happened to have been born Negro [...] I hope that every American, regardless of where he lives, will stop and examine his conscience about this and other related incidents. This nation was founded by men of many nations and backgrounds. It was founded on the principle that all men are created equal, and that the rights of every man are diminished when the rights of one man are threatened [...]

Today, we are committed to a worldwide struggle to promote and protect the rights of all who wish to be free. And when Americans are sent to Vietnam or West Berlin, we do not ask for whites only. It ought to be possible, therefore, for American students of any color to attend any public institution they select without having to be backed up by troops.

It ought to be possible for American consumers of any color to receive equal service in places of public accommodation, such as hotels and restaurants and theaters and retail stores, without being forced to resort to demonstrations in the street, and it ought to be possible for American citizens of any color to register to vote in a free election without interference or fear of reprisal.

It ought to be possible, in short, for every American to enjoy the privileges of being American without regard to his race or his color. In short, every American ought to have the right to be treated as he would wish to be treated, as one would wish his children to be treated. But this is not the case [...]

We preach freedom around the world, and we mean it, and we cherish our freedom here at home, but are we to say to the world, and much more importantly, to each other, that this is the land of the free except for the Negroes; that we have no second-class citizens except Negroes; that we have no class or caste system, no ghettoes, no master race except with respect to Negroes?

Now the time has come for this nation to fulfill its promise. The events in Birmingham and elsewhere have so increased the cries for equality that no city or State or legislative body can prudently choose to ignore them [...]

Next week, I shall ask the Congress of the United States to act, to make a commitment it has not fully made in this century to the proposition that race has no place in American life or law. The Federal judiciary has upheld that proposition in the conduct of its affairs, including the employment of Federal personnel, the use of Federal facilities, and the sale of federally financed housing [...]

I am [...] asking the Congress to enact legislation giving all Americans the right to be served in facilities which are open to the public – hotels, restaurants, theaters, retail stores, and similar establishments. This seems to me to be an elementary right. Its denial is an arbitrary indignity that no American in 1963 should have to endure, but many do.

I have recently met with scores of business leaders urging them to take voluntary action to end this discrimination and I have been encouraged by their response, and in the last two weeks over 75 cities have seen progress made in desegregating these kinds of facilities. But many are unwilling to act alone, and for this reason, nationwide legislation is needed if we are to move this problem from the streets to the courts.

I am also asking the Congress to authorize the Federal Government to participate more fully in lawsuits designed to end segregation in public education. We have succeeded in persuading many districts to desegregate voluntarily. Dozens have admitted Negroes without violence. Today, a Negro is attending a State-supported institution in every one of our 50 States, but the pace is very slow.

My fellow Americans, this is a problem which faces us all – in every city of the north as well as the south. Today there are Negroes unemployed, two or three times as many compared to whites, inadequate in education, moving into the large cities, unable to find work, young people particularly out of work without hope, denied equal rights, denied the opportunity to eat at a restaurant or lunch counter or go to a movie theater, denied the right to a decent education, denied almost today the right to attend a State university even though qualified [...]

We cannot say to ten percent of the population that you can't have that right; that your children cannot have the chance to develop whatever talents they have; that the only way that they are going to get their rights is to go into the streets and demonstrate. I think we owe them and we owe ourselves a better country than that.

Therefore, I am asking for your help in making it easier for us to move ahead and to provide the kind of equality of treatment which we would want ourselves; to give a chance for every child to be educated to the limit of his talents [...]

We have a right to expect that the Negro community will be responsible, will uphold the law, but they have a right to expect that the law will be fair, that the Constitution will be color blind, as Justice Harlan said at the turn of the century.

This is what we are talking about and this is a matter which concerns this country and what it stands for, and in meeting it I ask the support of all our citizens.

SPECIAL MESSAGE TO CONGRESS PROPOSING A NATIONWIDE WAR ON THE SOURCES OF POVERTY

Lyndon B. Johnson

1908–1973
36th President: November 22, 1963–January 20, 1969

On March 16, 1964, President Johnson launched the doctrine that was to become known as the War on Poverty. In the run-up to the 1964 presidential election, he pledged an expansion and an extension of help for the underpriveleged poor, with help for education and training and community-based initiatives. Further social reforms came in the following years with the introduction of Medicare and Medicaid and the civil-rights legislation that he had to force onto the southern states. However, his presidency will always be associated with the protests over the increasingly unpopular Vietnam War.

Because it is right, because it is wise, and because, for the first time in our history, it is possible to conquer poverty, I submit, for the consideration of the Congress and the country, the Economic Opportunity Act of 1964 [...]

It strikes at the causes, not just the consequences of poverty.

It can be a milestone in our 180-year search for a better life for our people.

This Act provides five basic opportunities.

It will give almost half a million underprivileged young Americans the opportunity to develop skills, continue education, and find useful work [...]

It will give dedicated Americans the opportunity to enlist as volunteers in the war against poverty.

It will give many workers and farmers the opportunity to break through particular barriers which bar their escape from poverty.

It will give the entire nation the opportunity for a concerted attack on poverty through the establishment, under my direction, of the Office of Economic Opportunity, a national headquarters for the war against poverty [...]

First, we will give high priority to helping young Americans who lack skills, who have not completed their education or who cannot complete it because they arc too poor [...]

I therefore recommend the creation of a Job Corps, a Work- Training Program, and a Work-Study Program.

A new national Job Corps will build toward an enlistment of 100,000 young men. They will be drawn from those whose background, health and education make them least fit for useful work [...]

Half of these young men will work, in the first year, on special conservation projects to give them education, useful work experience and to enrich the natural resources of the country.

Half of these young men will receive, in the first year, a blend of training, basic education and work experience in job Training Centers [...]

A new national Work-Training Program operated by the Department of Labour will provide work and training for 200,000 American men and women between the ages of 16 and 21. This will be developed through state and local governments and non-profit agencies [...]

A new national Work-Study Program operated by the Department of Health, Education, and Welfare will provide federal funds for part-time jobs for 140,000 young Americans who do not go to college because they cannot afford it.

There is no more senseless waste than the waste of the brainpower and skill of those who are kept from college by economic circumstance. Under this program they will, in a great American tradition, be able to work their way through school [...]

Second, through a new Community Action program we intend to strike at poverty at its source – in the streets of our cities and on the farms of our countryside among the very young and the impoverished old.

This program asks men and women throughout the country to prepare long-range plans for the attack on poverty in their own local communities [...]

Third, I ask for the authority to recruit and train skilled volunteers for the war against poverty.

Thousands of Americans have volunteered to serve the needs of other lands.

Thousands more want the chance to serve the needs of their own land.

They should have that chance.

Among older people who have retired, as well as among the young, among women as well as men, there are many Americans who are ready to enlist in our war against poverty.

They have skills and dedication. They are badly needed [...]

Fourth, we intend to create new opportunities for certain hard-hit groups to break out of the pattern of poverty.

Through a new program of loans and guarantees we can provide incentives to those who will employ the unemployed.

Through programs of work and retraining for unemployed fathers and mothers we can help them support their families in dignity while preparing themselves for new work.

Through funds to purchase needed land, organize cooperatives, and create new and adequate family farms we can help those whose life on the land has been a struggle without hope.

Fifth, I do not intend that the war against poverty become a series of uncoordinated and unrelated efforts – that it perish for lack of leadership and direction [...]

What you are being asked to consider is not a simple or an easy program. But poverty is not a simple or an easy enemy.

It cannot be driven from the land by a single attack on a single front. Were this so we would have conquered poverty long ago.

Nor can it be conquered by government alone [...]

Today, for the first time in our history, we have the power to strike away the barriers to full participation in our society. Having the power, we have the duty [...]

[...] This program will show the way to new opportunities for millions of our fellow citizens.

It will provide a lever with which we can begin to open the door to our prosperity for those who have been kept outside.

It will also give us the chance to test our weapons, to try our energy and ideas and imagination for the many battles yet to come. As conditions change, and as experience illuminates our difficulties, we will be prepared to modify our strategy.

And this program is much more than a beginning.

Rather it is a commitment. It is a total commitment by this President, and this

Congress, and this nation, to pursue victory over the most ancient of mankind's enemies.

SPEECH BEFORE CONGRESS ON VOTING RIGHTS

Lyndon B. Johnson

1908–1973
36th President: November 22, 1963–January 20, 1969

Early in 1965, civil-rights leaders chose Selma, Alabama, to break down the discriminatory voter-registration practices prevalent across the state that meant that while 99 percent of white adults were registered to vote, hardly any African-Americans were. In January, hundreds of voters lined up to register, but many were disqualified for minor mistakes on registration forms or on other spurious grounds. Various marches also took place, although an ordinance was introduced to prevent unlicensed marches. The event known as Bloody Sunday occurred on March 7, 1965 at the beginning of a planned march to Montgomery, when marchers refused to turn back from the Edmund Pettus Bridge and were whipped, beaten and repelled with tear gas.

[…] I speak tonight for the dignity of man and the destiny of democracy. I urge every member of both parties, Americans of all religions and of all colors, from every section of this country, to join me in that cause. At times history and fate meet at a single time in a single place to shape a turning point in man's unending search for freedom. So it was at Lexington and Concord. So it was a century ago at Appomattox. So it was last week in Selma, Alabama. There, long-suffering men and women peacefully protested the denial of their rights as Americans. Many were brutally assaulted. One good man, a man of God, was killed. There is no cause for pride in what has happened in Selma. There is no cause for self-satisfaction in the long denial of equal rights of millions of Americans. But there is cause for hope and for faith in our democracy in what is happening here tonight […]

Many of the issues of civil rights are very complex and most difficult. But about this there can and should be no argument. Every American citizen must have an equal right to vote. There is no reason which can excuse the denial of that right. There is no duty which weighs more heavily on us than the duty we have to ensure that right.

Yet the harsh fact is that in many places in this country men and women are kept from voting simply because they are Negroes [...]

In such a case our duty must be clear to all of us. The Constitution says that no person shall be kept from voting because of his race or his color. We have all sworn an oath before God to support and to defend that Constitution. We must now act in obedience to that oath.

Wednesday, I will send to Congress a law designed to eliminate illegal barriers to the right to vote. I have had prepared a more comprehensive analysis of the legislation which I had intended to transmit to the clerk tomorrow but which I will submit to the clerks tonight. But I want to really discuss with you now briefly the main proposals of this legislation.

This bill will strike down restrictions to voting in all elections – Federal, State, and local – which have been used to deny Negroes the right to vote.

This bill will establish a simple, uniform standard which cannot be used, however ingenious the effort, to flout our Constitution.

It will provide for citizens to be registered by officials of the United States Government if the State officials refuse to register them.

It will eliminate tedious, unnecessary lawsuits which delay the right to vote.

Finally, this legislation will ensure that properly registered individuals are not prohibited from voting [...]

To those who seek to avoid action by their National Government in their own communities; who want to and who seek to maintain purely local control over elections, the answer is simple:

Open your polling places to all your people.

Allow men and women to register and vote whatever the color of their skin.

Extend the rights of citizenship to every citizen of this land.

There is no constitutional issue here. The command of the Constitution is plain.

There is no moral issue. It is wrong – deadly wrong – to deny any of your fellow Americans the right to vote in this country.

There is no issue of States rights or national rights. There is only the struggle for human rights.

I have not the slightest doubt what will be your answer [...]

[...] there must be no delay, no hesitation and no compromise with our purpose.

We cannot, we must not, refuse to protect the right of every American to vote in every election that he may desire to participate in. And we ought not and we cannot and we must not wait another eight months before we get a bill. We have already waited a hundred years and more, and the time for waiting is gone [...]

Their cause must be our cause too. Because it is not just Negroes, but really it is all of us, who must overcome the crippling legacy of bigotry and injustice.

And we shall overcome [...]

But a century has passed, more than a hundred years, since the Negro was freed.

And he is not fully free tonight. It was more than a hundred years ago that Abraham Lincoln, a great President of another party, signed the Emancipation Proclamation, but emancipation is a proclamation and not a fact.

A century has passed, more than a hundred years, since equality was promised. And yet the Negro is not equal.

A century has passed since the day of promise. And the promise is unkept.

The time of justice has now come. I tell you that I believe sincerely that no force can hold it back. It is right in the eyes of man and God that it should come. And when it does, I think that day will brighten the lives of every American [...]

So I say to all of you here, and to all in the Nation tonight, that those who appeal to you to hold on to the past do so at the cost of denying you your future.

This great, rich, restless country can offer opportunity and education and hope to all: black and white, north and nouth, sharecropper and city dweller. These are the enemies: poverty, ignorance, disease. They are the enemies and not our fellow man, not our neighbor. And these enemies too, poverty, disease and ignorance, we shall overcome [...]

The real hero of this struggle is the American Negro. His actions and protests, his courage to risk safety and even to risk his life, have awakened the conscience of this Nation. His demonstrations have been designed to call attention to injustice, designed to provoke change, designed to stir reform [...]

For at the real heart of battle for equality is a deep-seated belief in the democratic process. Equality depends not on the force of arms or tear gas but upon the force of moral right [...]

There have been many pressures upon your President and there will be others as the days come and go. But I pledge you tonight that we intend to fight this battle where it should be fought: in the courts, and in the Congress, and in the hearts of men [...]

In Selma tonight, as in every [...] as in every city, we are working for just and peaceful settlement. We must all remember that after this speech I am making tonight, after the police and the FBI and the Marshals have all gone, and after you have promptly passed this bill, the people of Selma and the other cities of the nation must still live and work together. And when the attention of the nation has gone elsewhere they must try to heal the wounds and to build a new community [...]

I want to be the President who educated young children to the wonders of their world. I want to be the President who helped to feed the hungry and to prepare them to be taxpayers instead of taxeaters.

I want to be the President who helped the poor to find their own way and who protected the right of every citizen to vote in every election.

I want to be the President who helped to end hatred among his fellow men and who promoted love among the people of all races and all regions and all parties.

I want to be the President who helped to end war among the brothers of this earth.

[...] I came here tonight – not as President Roosevelt came down one time [...] to veto a bonus bill, not as President Truman came down one time to urge the passage of a railroad bill – but I came down here to ask you to share this task with me and to share it with the people that we both work for. I want this to be the Congress, Republicans and Democrats alike, which did all these things for all these people [...]

Above the pyramid on the great seal of the United States it says – in Latin – God has favored our undertaking.

God will not favor everything that we do. It is rather our duty to divine His will. But I cannot help believing that He truly understands and that He really favors the undertaking that we begin here tonight.

It was more than a hundred years ago that Abraham Lincoln, a great President of another party, signed the Emancipation Proclamation, but emancipation is a proclamation and not a fact.

A century has passed, more than a hundred years, since equality was promised. And yet the Negro is not equal.

A century has passed since the day of promise. And the promise is unkept. The time of justice has now come. I tell you that I believe sincerely that no force can hold it back. It is right in the eyes of man and God that it should come. And when it does, I think that day will brighten the lives of every American [...]

POLITICS & WAR

THE GETTYSBURG ADDRESS

Abraham Lincoln

1809–1865
16th President: 4 March 1861–15 April 1865

On November 19, 1863, during the dedication ceremony for the Soldiers' National Cemetery, President Lincoln gave a two-minute speech that has become one of the best-known in American history. Just four-and-a-half months after the Civil War battle at Gettysburg, in which thousands upon thousands of men had died for their causes, he redefined the Civil War as a struggle for freedom, not just a battle between states, invoked the spirit of the Declaration of Independence's call for equality and called for increased dedication from all so that the deaths of so many people were not in vain.

Four score and seven years ago our fathers brought forth, on this continent, a new nation, conceived in Liberty, and dedicated to the proposition that all men are created equal. Now we are engaged in a great civil war, testing whether that nation, or any nation so conceived and so dedicated, can long endure. We are met on a great battle-field of that war. We have come to dedicate a portion of that field, as a final resting place for those who here gave their lives that that nation might live. It is altogether fitting and proper that we should do this.

But, in a larger sense, we can not dedicate – we can not consecrate – we can not hallow – this ground. The brave men, living and dead, who struggled here, have consecrated it, far above our poor power to add or detract. The world will little note, nor long remember what we say here, but it can never forget what they did here.

It is for us the living, rather, to be dedicated here to the unfinished work which they who fought here have thus far so nobly advanced. It is rather for us to be here dedicated to the great task remaining before us – that from these honored dead we take increased devotion to that cause for which they here gave the last full measure of devotion – that we here highly resolve that these dead shall not have died in vain – that this nation, under God, shall have a new birth of freedom – and that government of the people, by the people, for the people, shall not perish from the earth.

DECORATION DAY SPEECH

James A. Garfield

1831–1881
20th President: March 4, 1881–September 19, 1881

James A. Garfield lasted only six months in office before being assassinated by Charles J. Guiteau, who was embittered after Garfield rejected a number of his applications for jobs and political posts. Garfield therefore had limited opportunity to make a mark, and his inauguration speech was considered to have been hastily written, and to fall flat. However, he was considered to be a skilled orator under other circumstances, and on the occasion of the first Memorial Day – known then as Decoration Day – Garfield, then a Republican Congressman, delivered this memorable line.

If silence is ever golden, it must be beside the graves of 15,000 men, whose lives were more significant than speech, and whose death was a poem the music of which can never be sung.

ADDRESS AT MINNESOTA STATE FAIR

Theodore Roosevelt

1858–1919
26th President: September 14, 1901–March 4, 1909

Theodore Roosevelt's robust but pragmatic attitude to foreign policy can be summed up in these two quotations from a speech that he gave at the opening of the Minnesota State Fair in September 1901, just 12 days before the assassination of President McKinley elevated him to the Oval Office. It comes originally from a West African proverb. He was specifically referring to the need to talk diplomatically to other governments but to build up and keep an effective, efficient navy so that the ideas of the Monroe Doctrine (aimed at preventing European interference in the Americas, i.e., in what the U.S. saw as its sphere of influence) could be implemented.

Speak softly, and carry a big stick. Right here let me make as vigorous a plea as I know how in favor of saying nothing that we do not mean, and of acting without hesitation up to whatever we say. A good many of you are probably acquainted with the old proverb, "Speak softly and carry a big stick – you will go far." If a man continually blusters, if he lacks civility, a big stick will not save him from trouble, and neither will speaking softly avail, if back of the softness there does not lie strength, power. In private life there are few beings more obnoxious than the man who is always loudly boasting, and if the boaster is not prepared to back up his words, his position becomes absolutely contemptible. So it is with the nation. It is both foolish and undignified to indulge in undue self-glorification, and, above all, in loose-tongued denunciation of other peoples. Whenever on any point we come in contact with a foreign power, I hope that we shall always strive to speak courteously and respectfully of that foreign power […]

Let us make it evident that we intend to do justice. Then let us make it equally evident that we will not tolerate injustice being done us in return. Let us further make it evident that we use no words which we are not which prepared to back up with deeds, and that while our speech is always moderate, we are ready and willing to make it good. Such an attitude will be the surest possible guarantee of that self-respecting peace, the attainment of which is and must ever be the prime aim of a self-governing people.

ADDRESS TO THE U.S. SENATE: "A WORLD LEAGUE FOR PEACE"

Woodrow Wilson

1856–1924
28th President: March 4, 1913–March 4, 1921

On January 22, 1917, President Wilson addressed the Senate, saying that he had had communications with representatives from both sides in Europe. He outlined the need for "peace without victory" where no party would feel overly aggrieved, all countries would be equal in rights and people would not be forced to swap from one power to another. The ideas in this speech would emerge in a more concrete form in the Fourteen Points of Peace speech the following year. The idea of not inflicting a humiliating defeat on Germany did not appeal to the French, and the subsequent punitive reparations and restrictions on armaments that were imposed caused resentment among Germans and the growth of groups such as the Nazis.

On the eighteenth of December, last I addressed an identic note to the governments of the nations now at war requesting them to state, more definitely than they had yet been stated by either group of belligerents, the terms upon which they would deem it possible to make peace. I spoke on behalf of humanity and of the rights of all neutral nations like our own, many of whose most vital interests the war puts in constant jeopardy. The Central Powers united in a reply which stated merely that they were ready to meet their antagonists in conference to discuss terms of peace.

The Entente Powers have replied much more definitely and have stated, in general terms, indeed, but with sufficient definiteness to imply details, the arrangements, guarantees, and acts of reparation which they deem to be the indispensable conditions of a satisfactory settlement. We are that much nearer a definite discussion of the peace which shall end the present war. We are that much nearer the discussion of the international concert which must thereafter hold the world at peace. In every discussion of the peace that must end this war it is taken for granted that that peace must be followed by some definite concert of power which will make it virtually impossible that any such catastrophe should ever overwhelm us again. Every lover of mankind, every sane and thoughtful man must take that for granted.

I have sought this opportunity to address you because I thought that I owed it to you, as the council associated with me in the final determination of our international obligations, to disclose to you without reserve the thought and purpose that have been taking form in my mind in regard to the duty of our Government in the days to come when it will be necessary to lay afresh and upon a new plan the foundations of peace among the nations.

It is inconceivable that the people of the United States should play no part in that great enterprise. To take part in such a service will be the opportunity for which they have sought to prepare themselves by the very principles and purposes of their polity and the approved practices of their Government ever since the days when they set up a new nation in the high and honorable hope that it might in all that it was and did show mankind the way to liberty. They cannot in honor withhold the service to which they are now about to be challenged. They do not wish to withhold it. But they owe it to themselves and to the other nations of the world to state the conditions under which they will feel free to render it.

That service is nothing less than this, to add their authority and their power to the authority and force of other nations to guarantee peace and justice throughout the world. Such a settlement cannot now be long postponed. It is right that before it comes this Government should frankly formulate the conditions upon which it would feel justified in asking our people to approve its formal and solemn adherence to a League for Peace. I am here to attempt to state those conditions.

The present war must first be ended; but we owe it to candour and to a just regard for the opinion of mankind to say that, so far as our participation in guarantees of future peace is concerned, it makes a great deal of difference in what way and upon what terms it is ended. The treaties and agreements which bring it to an end must embody terms which will create a peace that is worth guaranteeing and preserving, a peace that will win the approval of mankind, not merely a peace that will serve the several interests and immediate aims of the nations engaged. We shall have no voice in determining what those terms shall be, but we shall, I feel sure, have a voice in determining whether they shall be made lasting or not by the guarantees of a universal covenant; and our judgment upon what is fundamental and essential as a condition precedent to permanency should be spoken now, not afterwards when it may be too late.

No covenant of cooperative peace that does not include the peoples of the New World can suffice to keep the future safe against war; and yet there is only one sort of peace that the peoples of America could join in guaranteeing. The elements of that peace must be elements that engage the confidence and satisfy the principles of the American governments, elements consistent with their political faith and with the practical convictions which the peoples of America have once for all embraced and undertaken to defend [...]

ADDRESS TO A JOINT SESSION OF CONGRESS REQUESTING A DECLARATION OF WAR AGAINST GERMANY

Woodrow Wilson

1856–1924
28th President: March 4, 1913–March 4, 1921

While there was carnage on land for the whole of World War I, at sea the Allies had kept the German Fleet more or less confined to harbor. However, all shipping was vulnerable to attack by German submarines, especially the large convoys bringing supplies from across the Atlantic. Under pressure from the American government, Germany had stopped attacking neutral shipping, but resumed in February 1917. This, combined with an approach to Mexico to ask if it would attack America, guaranteed that America would join the Allies. On April 2, President Wilson asked Congress to approve his decision to go to war, which they did two days later.

[...] On the third of February last I officially laid before you the extraordinary announcement of the Imperial German Government that on and after the first day of Feburary it was its purpose to put aside all restraints of law or of humanity and use its submarines to sink every vessel that sought to approach either the ports of Great Britain and Ireland or the western coasts of Europe or any of the ports controlled by the enemies of Germany with the Mediterranean. That had seemed to be the object of the German submarine warfare earlier in the war, but since April of last year the Imperial Government had somewhat restrained the commanders of its undersea craft in conformity with its promise then given to us that passenger boats should not be sunk and that due warning would be given to all other vessels which its submarines might seek to destroy, when no resistance was offered or escape attempted, and care taken that their crews were given at least a fair chance to save their lives in their open boats. The precautions taken were meagre and haphazard enough, as was proved in distressing instance after instance in the progress of the cruel and unmanly business, but a certain degree of restraint was observed. The new policy has swept every restriction aside. Vessels of every kind, whatever their flag, their character, their cargo, their destination, their errand, have been ruthlessly sent to the bottom without warning and without
thought of help or mercy for those on board [...]
    [...] It is a war against all nations. American ships have been sunk, American lives taken, in ways which it has stirred us very deeply to learn of, but the ships and people of other neutral and friendly nations have been sunk and overwhelmed in the waters in the same way. There has been no discrimination. The challenge is to all mankind. Each nation must decide for itself how it will meet it. The choice we make for ourselves must be made with a moderation of counsel and a temperateness of judgment befitting our character and our motives as a nation. We must put excited feeling away. Our motive will not be revenge or the

victorious assertion of the physical might of the nation, but only the vindication of right, of human right, of which we are only a single champion.

With a profound sense of the solemn and even tragical character of the step I am taking and of the very grave responsibilities which it involves, but in unhesitating obedience to what I deem my constitutional duty, I advise that the Congress declare the recent course of the Imperial German Government to be in fact nothing less than war against the government and people of the United States; that it formally accept the status of belligerent which has thus been thrust upon it; and that it take immediate steps not only to put the country in a more thorough state of defense but also to exert all its power and employ all its resources to bring the Government of the German Empire to terms and end the war […]

It is a distressing and oppressive duty, Gentlemen of Congress, which I have performed in thus addressing you. There are, it may be, many months of fiery trial and sacrifice ahead of us. It is a fearful thing to lead this great and peaceful people into war, into the most terrible and disastrous of all wars, civilization itself seeming to be in the balance. But the right is more precious than peace, and we shall fight for the things which we have always carried nearest our hearts – for democracy, for the right of those who submit to authority to have a voice in their own governments, for the rights and liberties of small nations, for a universal dominion of right by such a concert of free peoples as shall bring peace and safety to all nations and make the world itself at last free. To such a task we can dedicate our lives and our fortunes, everything that we are and everything that we have, with the pride of those who know that the day has come when America is privileged to spend her blood and her might for the principles that gave her birth and happiness and the peace which she has treasured. God helping her, she can do no other.

THE FOURTEEN POINTS

Woodrow Wilson

—————— ••◆•• ——————

1856–1924

28th President: March 4, 1913–March 4, 1921

With the increased numbers of troops and firepower granted by American participation, the tide of World War I turned in 1917. On January 8, just over ten months before the Armistice, President Wilson set out in a speech – from which the long preamble and closing remarks are omitted here – to a joint session of Congress the terms for the surrender of the Central Powers. It is known as the Fourteen Points for Peace, or just Fourteen Points. The points include practicalities such as which territories should be returned to their previous nations and aspirational ideas for the formation of new countries out of the Austro-Hungarian and Ottoman Empires, freedom of the seas for all, open trade and peaceable relations between all countries. The negotiations for the Versailles Treaty compromised on many of these because other leaders saw them as unachieveable. Because of this, Senate did not ratify the treaty and the U.S. did not join the League of Nations.

I. Open covenants of peace, openly arrived at, after which there shall be no private international understandings of any kind but diplomacy shall proceed always frankly and in the public view.

II. Absolute freedom of navigation upon the seas, outside territorial waters, alike in peace and in war, except as the seas may be closed in whole or in part by international action for the enforcement of international covenants.

III. The removal, so far as possible, of all economic barriers and the establishment of an equality of trade conditions among all the nations consenting to the peace and associating themselves for its maintenance.

IV. Adequate guarantees given and taken that national armaments will be reduced to the lowest point consistent with domestic safety.

V. A free, open-minded, and absolutely impartial adjustment of all colonial claims, based upon a strict observance of the principle that in determining all such questions of sovereignty the interests of the populations concerned must have equal weight with the equitable claims of the government whose title is to be determined.

VI. The evacuation of all Russian territory and such a settlement of all questions affecting Russia as will secure the best and freest cooperation of the other nations of the world in obtaining for her an unhampered and unembarrassed opportunity for the independent determination of her own political development and national policy and assure her of a sincere welcome into the society of free nations under institutions of her own choosing; and, more than a welcome, assistance also of every kind that she may need and may herself desire. The treatment accorded Russia by her sister nations in the months to come will be the acid test of their good will, of their comprehension of her needs as distinguished from their own interests, and of their intelligent and unselfish sympathy.

VII. Belgium, the whole world will agree, must be evacuated and restored, without any attempt to limit the sovereignty which she enjoys in common with all other free nations. No other single act will serve as this will serve to restore confidence among the nations in the laws which they have themselves set and determined for the government of their relations with one another. Without this healing act the whole structure and validity of international law is forever impaired.

VIII. All French territory should be freed and the invaded portions restored, and the wrong done to France by Prussia in 1871 in the matter of Alsace-Lorraine, which has unsettled the peace of the world for nearly fifty years, should be righted, in order that peace may once more be made secure in the interest of all.

IX. A readjustment of the frontiers of Italy should be effected along clearly recognizable lines of nationality.

X. The peoples of Austria-Hungary, whose place among the nations we wish to see safeguarded and assured, should be accorded the freest opportunity of autonomous development.

XI. Rumania, Serbia, and Montenegro should be evacuated; occupied territories restored; Serbia accorded free and secure access to the sea; and the relations of the several Balkan states to one another determined by friendly counsel along historically established lines of allegiance and nationality; and international guarantees of the political and economic independence and territorial integrity of the several Balkan states should be entered into.

XII. The Turkish portions of the present Ottoman Empire should be assured a secure sovereignty, but the other nationalities which are now under Turkish rule should be assured an undoubted security of life and an absolutely unmolested opportunity of autonomous development, and the Dardanelles should be permanently opened as a free passage to the ships and commerce of all nations under international guarantees.

XIII. An independent Polish state should be erected which should include the territories inhabited by indisputably Polish populations, which should be assured a free and secure access to the sea, and whose political and economic independence and territorial integrity should be guaranteed by international covenant.

XIV. A general association of nations must be formed under specific covenants for the purpose of affording mutual guarantees of political independence and territorial integrity to great and small states alike. In regard to these essential rectifications of wrong and assertions of right we feel ourselves to be intimate partners of all the governments and peoples associated together against the Imperialists. We cannot be separated in interest or divided in purpose. We stand together until the end.

ADDRESS AT CHAUTAUQUA

Franklin D. Roosevelt

1882–1945
32nd President: March 4, 1933–April 12, 1945

During the presidential election campaign of 1936, President Roosevelt toured widely and, in August, returned to one of his favorite stomping grounds, Chautauqua, New York. In a speech that defined his foreign policy for most of his second term, the need for peaceful relations with other countries, including his "good-neighbor" policy with regard to the countries to the south, and neutrality for countries farther away. The "weapons" he describes as having been given to him by Congress are the first Neutrality Acts, which enabled him to embargo the sales of armaments to "belligerent" nations and in some cases travel to them.

As many of you who are here tonight know, I formed the excellent habit of coming to Chautauqua more than 20 years ago. After my inauguration in 1933, I promised Mr. Bestor that during the next four years I would come to Chautauqua again; it is in fulfillment of this that I am with you tonight.

A few days ago, I was asked what the subject of this talk would be, and I replied that for two good reasons I wanted to discuss the subject of peace. First, because it is eminently appropriate in Chautauqua; and, secondly, because in the hurly-burly of domestic politics it is important that our people should not overlook problems and issues which, though they lie beyond our borders, may, and probably will, have a vital influence on the United States of the future.

I say this to you not as a confirmed pessimist but as one who still hopes that envy, hatred, and malice among nations have reached their peak and will be succeeded by a new tide of peace and good will. I say this as one who has participated in many of the decisions of peace and war before, during, and after the World War; one who has traveled much, and one who has spent a goodly portion of every 24 hours in the study of foreign relations.

Long before I returned to Washington as President of the United States, I had made up my mind that, pending what might be called a more opportune moment on other continents, the United States could best serve the cause of a peaceful humanity by setting an example. That was why on March 4, 1933, I made the following declaration.

"In the field of world policy I would dedicate this nation to the policy of the good neighbor – the neighbor who resolutely respects himself and, because he does so, respects the rights of others – the neighbor who respects his obligations and respects the sanctity of his agreements in and with a world of neighbors."

This declaration represents my purpose; but it represents more than a purpose, for it stands for a practice […] the whole world now knows that the United States cherishes no predatory ambitions. We are strong; but less powerful nations know that they need not fear our strength. We seek no conquest: we stand for peace. In the whole of the Western hemisphere our good-neighbor policy has produced results that are especially heartening.

The noblest monument to peace and to neighborly economic and social friendship in all the world is not a monument in bronze or stone, but the boundary which unites the United States and Canada – 3,000 miles of friendship with no barbed wire, no gun or soldier, and no passport on the whole frontier. Mutual trust made that frontier. To extend the same sort of mutual trust throughout the Americas was our aim.

The American republics to the south of us have been ready always to cooperate with the United States on a basis of equality and mutual respect, but before we inaugurated the good-neighbor policy there was among them resentment and fear because certain administrations in Washington had slighted their national pride and their sovereign rights [...]

Peace, like charity, begins at home; that is why we have begun at home. But peace in the western world is not all that we seek.

It is our hope that knowledge of the practical application of the good-neighbor policy in this hemisphere will be borne home to our neighbors across the seas [...]

For ourselves we are on good terms with them – terms in most cases of straightforward friendship, of peaceful understanding.

But, of necessity, we are deeply concerned about tendencies of recent years among many of the nations of other continents. It is a bitter experience to us when the spirit of agreements to which we are a party is not lived up to. It is an even more bitter experience for the whole company of nations to witness not only the spirit but the letter of international agreements violated with impunity and without regard to the simple principles of honor. Permanent friendships between nations as between men can be sustained only by scrupulous respect for the pledged word [...]

We are not isolationists except insofar as we seek to isolate ourselves completely from war. Yet we must remember that so long as war exists on Earth there will be some danger that even the nation which most ardently desires peace may be drawn into war [...]

I wish I could keep war from all nations, but that is beyond my power. I can at least make certain that no act of the United States helps to produce or to promote war. I can at least make clear that the conscience of America revolts against war and that any nation which provokes war forfeits the sympathy of the people of the United States [...]

In one field, that of economic barriers, the American policy may be, I hope, of some assistance in discouraging the economic source of war and therefore a contribution toward the peace of the world. The trade agreements which we are making are not only finding outlets for the products of American fields and

American factories but are also pointing the way to the elimination of embargoes, quotas, and other devices which place such pressure on nations not possessing great natural resources that to them the price of peace seems less terrible than the price of war.

The Congress of the United States has given me certain authority to provide safeguards of American neutrality in case of war.

The President of the United States who, under our Constitution, is vested with primary authority to conduct our international relations, thus has been given new weapons with which to maintain our neutrality. Nevertheless – and I speak from a long experience – the effective maintenance of American neutrality
depends today, as in the past, on the wisdom and determination of whoever at the moment occupy the offices of President and Secretary of State [...]

We seek to dominate no other nation. We ask no territorial expansion. We oppose imperialism. We desire reduction in world armaments.

We believe in democracy; we believe in freedom; we believe in peace. We offer to every nation of the world the handclasp of good neighbor. Let those who wish our friendship look us in eye and take our hand.

THE ATLANTIC CHARTER

Franklin D. Roosevelt
with Winston Churchill

1882–1945
32nd President: March 4, 1933–April 12, 1945

The Atlantic Charter was an agreement drawn up between the U.S.A. and U.K. that forms the basis for many post-World War II international agreements. It set out the premise that neither country would make territorial gains after the war (this may have been included because the American President distrusted British imperial ambitions) and the idea that all people should have the right to self-determination. Other measures included global economic co-operation, the lowering of trade barriers, disarmament of aggressor nations among a general disarmament that would come with the end of war, freedom of the seas, human rights and increased social welfare.

The President of the United States and the Prime Minister, Mr. Churchill, representing His Majesty's Government in the United Kingdom, have met at sea.

They have been accompanied by officials of their two governments, including high ranking officers of the Military, Naval and Air Services.

The whole problem of the supply of munitions of war, as provided by the Lease-Lend Act, for the armed forces of the United States and for those countries actively engaged in resisting aggression has been further examined.

Lord Beaverbrook, the Minister of Supply of the British Government, has joined in these conferences. He is going to proceed to Washington to discuss further details with appropriate officials of the United States Government. These conferences will also cover the supply problems of the Soviet Union.

The President and the Prime Minister have had several conferences They have considered the dangers to world civilization arising from the policies of military domination by conquest upon which the Hitlerite government of Germany and other governments associated therewith have embarked, and have made clear the stress which their countries are respectively taking for their safety in the face of these dangers.

They have agreed upon the following joint declaration: Joint declaration of the President of the United States of America and the Prime Minister, Mr. Churchill, representing His Majesty's Government in the United Kingdom, being met together, deem it right to make known certain common principles in the national policies of their respective countries on which they base their hopes for a better future for the world.

First, their countries seek no aggrandizement, territorial or other;

Second, they desire to see no territorial changes that do not accord with the freely expressed wishes of the peoples concerned;

Third, they respect the right of all peoples to choose the form of government under which they will live; and they wish to see sovereign rights and self-government restored to those who have been forcibly deprived of them;

Fourth, they will endeavor, with due respect for their existing obligations, to further the enjoyment by all States, great or small, victor or vanquished, of access, on equal terms, to the trade and to the raw materials of the world which are needed for their economic prosperity;

Fifth, they desire to bring about the fullest collaboration between all nations in the economic field with the object of securing, for all, improved labor standards, economic advancement and social security;

Sixth, after the final destruction of the Nazi tyranny, they hope to see established a peace which will afford to all nations the means of dwelling in safety within their own boundaries, and which will afford assurance that all the men in all the lands may live out their lives in freedom from fear and want;

Seventh, such a peace should enable all men to traverse the high seas and oceans without hindrance;

Eighth, they believe that all of the nations of the world, for realistic as well as spiritual reasons must come to the abandonment of the use of force. Since no future peace can be maintained if land, sea or air armaments continue to be employed by nations which threaten, or may threaten, aggression outside of their frontiers, they believe, pending the establishment of a wider and permanent system of general security, that the disarmament of such nations is essential. They will likewise aid and encourage all other practicable measures which will lighten for peace-loving peoples the crushing burden of armaments.

ADDRESS TO CONGRESS REQUESTING A DECLARATION OF WAR

Franklin D. Roosevelt

1882–1945
32nd President: March 4, 1933–April 12, 1945

The day after Japan attacked the U.S. Pacific Fleet's headquarters at Pearl Harbor, on Oahu, and several other targets across the Pacific, President Franklin D. Roosevelt addressed a Joint Session of Congress to ask them to declare war against Japan. The Japanese aim had been to destroy America's ability to deploy aircraft around the Pacific Ocean, but the aircraft carriers were out on manoeuvres and so escaped the attack. However, 300 aircraft and 18 ships were destroyed or damaged severely, 2,402 people were killed and 1,282 wounded. The Japanese had intended to prevent the Americans entering the war in the Pacific but instead precipitated it.

Yesterday, December 7, 1941 – a date which will live in infamy – the United States of America was suddenly and deliberately attacked by naval and air forces of the Empire of Japan.

The United States was at peace with that nation and, at the solicitation of Japan, was still in conversation with its government and its Emperor looking toward the maintenance of peace in the Pacific.

Indeed, one hour after Japanese air squadrons had commenced bombing in the American island of Oahu, the Japanese Ambassador to the United States and his colleague delivered to our Secretary of State a formal reply to a recent American message. And, while this reply stated that it seemed useless to continue the existing diplomatic negotiations, it contained no threat or hint of war or of armed attack [...]

The attack yesterday on the Hawaiian Islands has caused severe damage to American naval and military forces. I regret to tell you that very many American lives have been lost [...]

Yesterday, the Japanese Government also launched an attack against Malaya.

Last night Japanese forces attacked Hong Kong.
Last night Japanese forces attacked Guam.
Last night Japanese forces attacked the Philippine Islands.
Last night the Japanese attacked Wake Island.
And this morning the Japanese attacked Midway Island [...]

I believe that I interpret the will of the Congress and of the people when I assert that we will not only defend ourselves to the uttermost but will make it very certain that this form of treachery shall never again endanger us.

Hostilities exist. There is no blinking at the fact that our people, our territory and our interests are in grave danger.

With confidence in our armed forces, with the unbounding determination of our people, we will gain the inevitable triumph. So help us God.

I ask that the Congress declare that since the unprovoked and dastardly attack by Japan on Sunday, December 7, 1941, a state of war has existed between the United States and the Japanese Empire take our hand.

NOTE FOR SPEECH ON THE NORMANDY LANDINGS

Dwight D. Eisenhower

1890–1969
34th President: January 20, 1953–January 20, 1961

These notes for a speech that was never actually given offer a fascinating insight into the burdens of crisis leadership and the sense of personal responsibility that can combine to forge a truly great president. On June 5, 1944, General Dwight D. Eisenhower, who was to become one of America's most highly-regarded presidents, was holed up in a cottage in France, preparing for what would become known as the

Battle of Normandy. In case of defeat, he drafted the following note, underlining the words "mine alone" to emphasis that he took full responsibility for the decision. In the event, the invasion was a success, and the note never had to be used.

Our landings in the Cherbourg-Havre area have failed to gain a satisfactory foothold and I have withdrawn the troops. My decision to attack at this time and place was based upon the best information available. The troops, the air and the Navy did all that bravery and devotion to duty could do. If any blame or fault attaches to the attempt it is mine alone.

STATEMENT ANNOUNCING THE USE OF THE A-BOMB AT HIROSHIMA

Harry S. Truman

1884–1972
33rd President: April 12, 1945–January 20, 1953

When Vice President Harry S. Truman became President in April 1945, following the death of President Franklin D. Roosevelt, he did not know about the Manhattan Project and its plans to develop atomic and nuclear weapons. After the Axis Powers had been defeated in Europe in June, he turned his attention to the Far East, where war was still ongoing. Negotiations with the Japanese had been underway, but they did not accede to the Allies' demand for an unconditional surrender. The new President Truman then had the immediate choice of a quick strike or months of costly fighting. He chose the former option and, as a result, on August 6, the Enola Gay *dropped an atomic bomb on the city of Hiroshima.*

Sixteen hours ago an American airplane dropped one bomb on Hiroshima, an important Japanese army base. That bomb had more power than 20,000 tons of TNT. It had more than 2000 times the blast power of the British "Grand Slam', which is the largest bomb ever yet used in the history of warfare.

The Japanese began the war from the air at Pearl Harbor. They have been repaid manyfold. And the end is not yet. With this bomb we have now added a new and revolutionary increase in destruction to supplement the growing power of our armed forces. In their present form these bombs are now in production, and even more powerful forms are in development. It is an atomic bomb. It is a harnessing of the basic power of the universe. The force from which the Sun draws its power has been loosed against those who brought war to the Far East.

Before 1939, it was the accepted belief of scientists that it was theoretically possible to release atomic energy. But no one knew any practical method of doing it. By 1942, however, we knew that the Germans were working feverishly to find a way to add atomic energy to the other engines of war with which they hoped to enslave the world. But they failed. We may be grateful to Providence that the Germans got the V-1s and V-2s late and in limited quantities and even more grateful that they did not get the atomic bomb at all.

RECOGNITION OF THE STATE OF ISRAEL

Harry S. Truman

1884–1972
33rd President: April 12, 1945–January 20, 1953

After the Balfour Declaration of 1917, increasing numbers of Zionists had moved to Palestine, particularly in the light of the horrors of Nazi persecution in Europe. After

World War II, the mandated authority, Britain, turned the problem of conflicting Arab and Jewish aspirations over to the United Nations, which proposed partition, although this solution was rejected by the Arab majority. The armed Zionist forces won the ensuing civil war and on May 14, 1948, the State of Israel was proclaimed, and, eleven minutes later, President Harry S. Truman announced that the U.S. Government gave official recognition to the de facto government. Within 24 hours, Egypt, Iraq, Lebanon, Syria, and Transjordan invaded, in what was to be the first of the Arab-Israeli wars, and hundreds of thousands of Palestinians fled. More than 60 years later, there is still no solution.

This Government has been informed that a Jewish state has been proclaimed in Palestine, and recognition has been requested by the provisional Government thereof.

The United States recognizes the provisional government as the de facto authority of the new State of Israel.

"CHANCE FOR PEACE" SPEECH

Dwight D. Eisenhower

1890–1969
34th President: January 20, 1953–January 20, 1961

In one of his first major speeches after his inauguration – known as the "chance for peace" – President Dwight D. Eisenhower spoke to the American Society of Newspaper Editors on April 16, 1953. As Supreme Allied Commander in Europe during World War II and a veteran of World War I, he had seen enough war to last a lifetime and pledged to use the nation's wealth for better projects. Within weeks, he had signed the armistice that ended the Korean War and, by the end of the year, he outlined his proposals for a body concerned with nuclear cooperation and monitoring, set up in 1957 as the "Atoms for Peace" organization – now the International Atomic Energy Agency (IAEA).

[...] In this spring of 1953 the free world weighs one question above all others: the chances for a just peace for all peoples. To weigh this chance is to summon instantly to mind another recent moment of great decision. It came with that yet more hopeful spring of 1945, bright with the promise of victory and of freedom. The hopes of all just men in that moment, too, was a just and lasting peace [...]

This common purpose lasted an instant and perished. The nations of the world divided to follow two distinct roads [...]

The way chosen by the United States was plainly marked by a few clear precepts, which govern its conduct in world affairs [...]

This way was faithful to the spirit that inspired the United Nations: to prohibit strife, to relieve tensions, to banish fears. This way was to control and to reduce armaments. This way was to allow all nations to devote their energies and resources to the great and good tasks of healing the war's wounds, of clothing and feeding and housing the needy, of perfecting a just political life, of enjoying the fruits of their own toil.

The Soviet government held a vastly different vision of the future. In the world of its design, security was to be found, not in mutual trust and mutual aid but in force: huge armies, subversion, rule of neighbor nations. The goal was power superiority at all cost. Security was to be sought by denying it to all others [...]

The amassing of Soviet power alerted free nations to a new danger of aggression.

It compelled them in self-defense to spend unprecedented money and energy for armaments. It forced them to develop weapons of war now capable of inflicting instant and terrible punishment upon any aggressor.

It instilled in the free nations [...] the unshakable conviction that, as long as there persists a threat to freedom, they must, at any cost, remain armed, strong, and ready for the risk of war. It inspired them – and let none doubt this – to attain a unity of purpose and will beyond the power of propaganda or pressure to break, now or ever [...]

The free nations, most solemnly and repeatedly, have assured the Soviet Union that their firm association has never had any aggressive purpose whatsoever. Soviet leaders, however, have seemed to persuade themselves, or tried to persuade their people, otherwise.

And so it has come to pass that the Soviet Union itself has shared and suffered the very fears it has fostered in the rest of the world [...]

What can the world, or any nation in it, hope for if no turning is found on this dread road?

The worst to be feared and the best to be expected can be simply stated.

The worst is atomic war.

The best would be this: a life of perpetual fear and tension; a burden of arms draining the wealth and the labor of all peoples; a wasting of strength that defies the American system or the Soviet system or any system to achieve true abundance and happiness for the peoples of this Earth [...]

This is one of those times in the affairs of nations when the gravest choices must be made, if there is to be a turning toward a just and lasting peace.

It is a moment that calls upon the governments of the world to speak their intentions with simplicity and with honesty.

It calls upon them to answer the question that stirs the hearts of all sane men: is there no other way the world may live? [...]

The free world knows, out of the bitter wisdom of experience, that vigilance and sacrifice are the price of liberty [...]

So the new Soviet leadership now has a precious opportunity to awaken, with the rest of the world, to the point of peril reached and to help turn the tide of history.

Will it do this?

We do not yet know. Recent statements and gestures of Soviet leaders give some evidence that they may recognize this critical moment [...]

As progress in all these areas strengthens world trust, we could proceed concurrently with the next great work – the reduction of the burden of armaments now weighing upon the world. To this end we would welcome and enter into the most solemn agreements [...]

The peace we seek, founded upon decent trust and cooperative effort among nations, can be fortified, not by weapons of war but by wheat and by cotton, by milk and by wool, by meat and timber and rice. These are words that translate into every language on Earth. These are the needs that challenge this world in arms [...]

We are prepared to reaffirm, with the most concrete evidence, our readiness to help build a world in which all peoples can be productive and prosperous [...]

I know of only one question upon which progress waits. It is this: What is the Soviet Union ready to do? [...]

[...] where then is the concrete evidence of the Soviet Union's concern for peace?

There is, before all peoples, a precarious chance to turn the black tide of events.

If we fail to strive to seize this chance, the judgment of future ages will be harsh and just.

If we strive but fail and the world remains armed against itself, it at least would need be divided no longer in its clear knowledge of who has condemned humankind to this fate.

The purpose of the United States, in stating these proposals, is simple. These proposals spring, without ulterior motive or political passion, from our calm conviction that the hunger for peace is in the hearts of all people – those of Russia and of China no less than of our own country.

They conform to our firm faith that God created man to enjoy, not destroy, the fruits of the Earth and of their own toil.

They aspire to this: the lifting, from the backs and from the hearts of men, of their burden of arms and of fears, so that they may find before them a golden age of freedom and of peace.

THE "SILENT MAJORITY" SPEECH

Richard Nixon

1913–1994
37th President: January 20, 1969–August 9, 1974

On November 3, 1969, President Richard Nixon gave a television broadcast to the nation, explaining – in the face of demonstrations and sometimes violent protests – why it would be wrong for the U.S. Government to pull out its troops from the Vietnam War. The three principles, known as the Nixon Doctrine, were announced in Guam and it was the third of those that he invoked as the reason behind remaining engaged in the Vietnam War.

Tonight, I want to talk to you on a subject of deep concern to all Americans and to many people in all parts of the world – the war in Vietnam.

I believe that one of the reasons for the deep division about Vietnam is that many Americans have lost confidence in what their Government has told them about our policy. The American people cannot and should not be asked to support a policy which involves the overriding issues of war and peace unless they know the truth about that policy [...]

Now, let me begin by describing the situation I found when I was inaugurated on January 20.

The war had been going on for four years.

31,000 Americans had been killed in action.

The training program for the South Vietnamese was behind schedule.

540,000 Americans were in Vietnam with no plans to reduce the number.

No progress had been made at the negotiations in Paris and the United States had not put forth a comprehensive peace proposal.

The war was causing deep division at home and criticism from many of our friends as well as our enemies abroad.

In view of these circumstances there were some who urged that I end the war at once by ordering the immediate withdrawal of all American forces [...]

[...] I had a greater obligation than to think only of the years of my administration and of the next election. I had to think of the effect of my decision on the next generation and on the future of peace and freedom in America and in the world [...]

The great question is: How can we win America's peace?

[...] Now that we are in the war, what is the best way to end it?

In January, I could only conclude that the precipitate withdrawal of American forces from Vietnam would be a disaster not only for South Vietnam but for the United States and for the cause of peace.

For the South Vietnamese, our precipitate withdrawal would inevitably allow the Communists to repeat the massacres which followed their takeover in the North 15 years before [...]

For the United States, this first defeat in our Nation's history would result in a collapse of confidence in American leadership, not only in Asia but throughout the world [...]

For the future of peace, precipitate withdrawal would thus be a disaster of immense magnitude. A nation cannot remain great if it betrays its allies and lets down its friends.

Our defeat and humiliation in South Vietnam without question would promote recklessness in the councils of those great powers who have not yet abandoned their goals of world conquest [...]

Ultimately, this would cost more lives.

It would not bring peace; it would bring more war.

For these reasons, I rejected the recommendation that I should end the war by immediately withdrawing all of our forces. I chose instead to change American policy on both the negotiating front and battle front [...]We have offered the complete withdrawal of all outside forces within one year.

We have proposed a cease-fire under international supervision.

We have offered free elections under international supervision with the Communists participating in the organization and conduct of the elections as an organized political force. And the Saigon Government has pledged to accept the result of the elections [...]

Hanoi has refused even to discuss our proposals. They demand our unconditional acceptance of their terms, which are that we withdraw all American forces immediately and unconditionally and that we overthrow the Government of South Vietnam as we leave [...]

Tonight, I am taking the unprecedented step of disclosing to you some of our other initiatives for peace – initiatives we undertook privately and secretly because we thought we thereby might open a door which publicly would be closed [...]

We have taken other significant initiatives which must remain secret to keep open some channels of communication which may still prove to be productive [...]

It has become clear that the obstacle in negotiating an end to the war is not the President of the United States. It is not the South Vietnamese Government.

The obstacle is the other side's absolute refusal to show the least willingness to join us in seeking a just peace. And it will not do so while it is convinced that all it has to do is to wait for our next concession, and our next concession after that one, until it gets everything it wants [...]

I realize that this report on our efforts on the diplomatic front is discouraging to the American people, but the American people are entitled to know the truth – the bad news as well as the good news where the lives of our young men are involved.

Now let me turn, however, to a more encouraging report on another front.

At the time we launched our search for peace, I recognized we might not succeed in bringing an end to the war through negotiation. I, therefore, put into effect another plan to bring peace – a plan which will bring the war to an end regardless of what happens on the negotiating front.

It is in line with a major shift in U.S. foreign policy which I described in my press conference at Guam on July 25. Let me briefly explain what has been described as the Nixon Doctrine – a policy which not only will help end the war in Vietnam, but which is an essential element of our program to prevent future Vietnams.

We Americans are a do-it-yourself people. We are an impatient people. Instead of teaching someone else to do a job, we like to do it ourselves. And this trait has been carried over into our foreign policy [...] Before any American troops were committed to Vietnam, a leader of another Asian country expressed this opinion to me when I was traveling in Asia as a private citizen. He said: "When you are trying to assist another nation defend its freedom, US policy should be to help them fight the war but not to fight the war for them."

Well, in accordance with this wise counsel, I laid down in Guam three principles as guidelines for future American policy toward Asia:

First, the United States will keep all of its treaty commitments;

Second, we shall provide a shield if a nuclear power threatens the freedom of a nation allied with us or of a nation whose survival we consider vital to our security;

Third, in cases involving other types of aggression, we shall furnish military and economic assistance when requested in accordance with our treaty commitments.

But we shall look to the nation directly threatened to assume the primary responsibility of providing the manpower for its defense [...]

The policy of the previous administration not only resulted in our assuming the primary responsibility for fighting the war, but even more significantly did not adequately stress the goal of strengthening the South Vietnamese so that they could defend themselves when we left.

The Vietnamization plan was launched following Secretary Laird's visit to Vietnam in March. Under the plan, I ordered first a substantial increase in the training and equipment of South Vietnamese forces. In July, on my visit to Vietnam, I changed General Abrams' orders so that they were consistent with the objectives of our new policies. Under the new orders, the primary mission of our troops is to enable the South Vietnamese forces to assume the full responsibility for the security of South Vietnam.

Our air operations have been reduced by over 20 percent.

And now we have begun to see the results of this long overdue change in American policy in Vietnam.

After five years of Americans going into Vietnam, we are finally bringing American men home. By December 15, over 60,000 men will have been withdrawn from South Vietnam – including 20 percent of all of our combat forces.

The South Vietnamese have continued to gain in strength. As a result they have been able to take over combat responsibilities from our American troops [...]

Most important – United States casualties have declined during the last two months to the lowest point in three years.

Let me now turn to our program for the future.

We have adopted a plan which we have worked out in cooperation with the South Vietnamese for the complete withdrawal of all U.S. combat ground forces, and their replacement by South Vietnamese forces on an orderly scheduled timetable. This withdrawal will be made from strength and not from weakness. As South Vietnamese forces become stronger, the rate of American withdrawal can become greater [...]

My fellow Americans, I am sure you can recognize from what I have said that we really only have two choices open to us if we want to end this war.

I can order an immediate, precipitate withdrawal of all Americans from Vietnam without regard to the effects of that action.

Or we can persist in our search for a just peace through a negotiated settlement if possible, or through continued implementation of our plan for Vietnamization if necessary – a plan in which we will withdraw all of our forces from Vietnam on a schedule in accordance with our program, as the South Vietnamese become strong enough to defend their own freedom.

I have chosen this second course.

It is not the easy way.

It is the right way.

It is a plan which will end the war and serve the cause of peace-not just in Vietnam but in the Pacific and in the world.

STATEMENT BY PRESIDENT KENNEDY ON RECEIPT OF CHAIRMAN KHRUSHCHEV'S LETTER

John F. Kennedy

1917–1963

35th President: January 20, 1961–November 22, 1963

Just a week after President John F. Kennedy had told the American public of the presence of Soviet missiles in Cuba, the immediate crisis was over. In a telex sent to Chairman Nikita Khrushchev at the same time, he said that America would no longer seek to interfere in Cuba's internal affairs, would respect its sovereignty and borders, and would not allow U.S. territory to be used by anyone else to invade Cuba. What was not made public was the American agreement to withdraw missiles from bases in Turkey. This angered Chairman Khrushchev, as it made it appear that the U.S.S.R. had backed down.

I welcome Chairman Khrushchev's statesmanlike decision to stop building bases in Cuba, dismantling offensive weapons and returning them to the Soviet Union under United Nations verification. This is an important and constructive contribution to peace.

We shall be in touch with the Secretary General of the United Nations with respect to reciprocal measures to assure peace in the Caribbean area.

It is my earnest hope that the governments of the world can, with a solution of the Cuban crisis, turn their urgent attention to the compelling necessity for ending the arms race and reducing world tensions. This applies to the military confrontation between the Warsaw Pact and NATO countries as well as to other situations in other parts of the world where tensions lead to the wasteful diversion of resources to weapons of war.

"ICH BIN EIN BERLINNER"

John F. Kennedy

1917–1963
35th President: January 20, 1961–November 22, 1963

Two years after the building of the Berlin Wall, President John F. Kennedy visited West Berlin, including a trip to the infamous Checkpoint Charlie, the most notorious crossing point on the wall. He was watched from the far side by small groups of East German citizens, standing under the watchful eye of state police.

Later that day, from a platform on the steps of the Rathaus – city hall – in front of an audience of 120,000 people, Kennedy delivered a defiant speech rebuffing the Soviet leadership's hopes of driving the Allies out of West Berlin. Two months later, President Kennedy and Chairman Krushchev negotiated the first nuclear test ban treaty between the U.S.A. and the U.S.S.R..

I am proud to come to this city as the guest of your distinguished Mayor, who has symbolized throughout the world the fighting spirit of West Berlin. And I am proud to visit the Federal Republic with your distinguished Chancellor who for so many years has committed Germany to democracy and freedom and progress, and to come here in the company of my fellow American, General Clay, who has been in this city during its great moments of crisis and will come again if ever needed.

Two thousand years ago the proudest boast was "civis Romanus sum." Today, in the world of freedom, the proudest boast is "Ich bin ein Berliner."

I appreciate my interpreter translating my German!

There are many people in the world who really don't understand, or say they don't, what is the great issue between the free world and the Communist world. Let them come to Berlin. There are some who say that communism is the wave of the future. Let them come to Berlin. And there are some who say in Europe and elsewhere we can work with the Communists. Let them come to Berlin. And there are even a few who say that it is true that communism is an evil system, but it it permits us to make economic progress. Lass' sie nach Berlin kommen. Let them come to Berlin.

Freedom has many difficulties and democracy is not perfect, but we have never had to put a wall up to keep our people in, to prevent them from leaving us. I want to say, on behalf of my countrymen, who live many miles away on the other side of the Atlantic, who are far distant from you, that they take the greatest pride that they have been able to share with you, even from a distance, the story of the last 18 years. I know of no town, no city, that has been besieged for 18 years that still lives with the vitality and the force, and the hope and the determination of the city of West Berlin. While the wall is the most obvious and vivid demonstration of the failures of the Communist system, for all the world to see, we take no satisfaction in it, for it is, as your Mayor has said, an offense not only against history but an offense against humanity, separating families, dividing husbands and wives and brothers and sisters, and dividing a people who wish to be joined together.

What is true of this city is true of Germany – real, lasting peace in Europe can never be assured as long as one German out of four is denied the elementary right of free men, and that is to make a free choice. In 18 years of peace and good faith, this generation of Germans has earned the right to be free, including the right to unite their families and their nation in lasting peace, with good will to all people. You live in a defended island of freedom, but your life is part of the main. So let me ask you as I close, to lift your eyes beyond the dangers of today, to the hopes of tomorrow, beyond the freedom merely of this city of Berlin, or your country of Germany, to the advance of freedom everywhere, beyond the wall to the day of peace with justice, beyond yourselves and ourselves to all mankind.

Freedom is indivisible, and when one man is enslaved, all are not free. When all are free, then we can look forward to that day when this city will be joined as one and this country and this great Continent of Europe in a peaceful and hopeful globe. When that day finally comes, as it will, the people of West Berlin can take sober satisfaction in the fact that they were in the front lines for almost two decades. All free men, wherever they may live, are citizens of Berlin, and, therefore, as a free man, I take pride in the words "Ich bin ein Berliner."

REPORT ON THE GULF OF TONKIN INCIDENT

Lyndon B. Johnson

1908–1973

36th President: November 22, 1963–January 20, 1969

In response to the Gulf of Tonkin incidents of August 2 and 4, 1964, in which U.S. naval vessels had reportedly been attacked in international waters, President Lyndon B. Johnson made a broadcast to the nation. He repeated his promise of there being "no wider war" and within days, Congress had passed the Southeast Asia Resolution, Public Law 88-408, which gave the president the power to use military force anywhere in southeast Asia and intervene in countries threatened by communist forces, without having to wait for a formal declaration of war by Congress.

My fellow Americans: As President and Commander in Chief, it is my duty to the American people to report that renewed hostile actions against United States ships on the high seas in the Gulf of Tonkin have today required me to order the military forces of the United States to take action in reply.

The initial attack on the destroyer Maddox, on August 2, was repeated today by a number of hostile vessels attacking two U.S. destroyers with torpedoes. The destroyers and supporting aircraft acted at once on the orders I gave after the initial act of aggression. We believe at least two of the attacking boats were sunk. There were no U.S. losses […]

In the larger sense this new act of aggression, aimed directly at our own forces, again brings home to all of us in the United States the importance of the struggle for peace and security in southeast Asia. Aggression by terror against the peaceful villagers of South Vietnam has now been joined by open aggression on the high seas against the United States of America […]

It is a solemn responsibility to have to order even limited military action by forces whose overall strength is as vast and as awesome as those of the United

States of America, but it is my considered conviction, shared throughout your Government, that firmness in the right is indispensable today for peace; that firmness will always be measured. Its mission is peace.

"A WAR THAT IS FINISHED"

Gerald Ford

1913–2006
38th President: August 9, 1974–January 20, 1977

In the Vietnam War, America supported the government of South Vietnam against the communist regime of the North, which was supported by the Soviet Union and China. The conflict began in November 1955, and by the spring of 1975 had become a protracted nightmare, having claimed the lives of 58,000 Americans, and over two million Vietnamese. As long ago as 1970, polls had shown that a third of Americans were strongly against the war and, by 1975, people, especially young men who were subject to the draft, were increasingly desperate simply for it to end.
Gerald Ford's speech of April 23, 1975, brought the news that people had both dreaded and longed for: withdrawal of U.S. troops. A week after the speech, the South Vietnamese capital of Saigon fell to the armies of the North.

On January 8, 1815, a monumental American victory was achieved here – the Battle of New Orleans. Louisiana had been a State for less than three years, but outnumbered Americans innovated, outnumbered Americans used the tactics of the frontier to defeat a veteran British force trained in the strategy of the Napoleonic wars.

We as a nation had suffered humiliation and a measure of defeat in the War of

1812. Our National Capital in Washington had been captured and burned. So, the illustrious victory in the Battle of New Orleans was a powerful restorative to our national pride.

Yet, the victory at New Orleans actually took place two weeks after the signing of the armistice in Europe. Thousands died although a peace had been negotiated. The combatants had not gotten the word. Yet, the epic struggle nevertheless restored America's pride.

Today, America can regain the sense of pride that existed before Vietnam. But it cannot be achieved by refighting a war that is finished as far as America is concerned. As I see it, the time has come to look forward to an agenda for the future, to unify, to bind up the Nation's wounds, and to restore its health and its optimistic self-confidence.

In New Orleans, a great battle was fought after a war was over. In New Orleans tonight, we can begin a great national reconciliation. The first engagement must be with the problems of today, but just as importantly, the problems of the future. That is why I think it is so appropriate that I find myself tonight at a university which addresses itself to preparing young people for the challenge of tomorrow.

I ask that we stop refighting the battles and the recriminations of the past. I ask that we look now at what is right with America, at our possibilities and our potentialities for change and growth and achievement and sharing. I ask that we accept the responsibilities of leadership as a good neighbor to all peoples and the enemy of none. I ask that we strive to become, in the finest American tradition, something more tomorrow than we are today.

Instead of my addressing the image of America, I prefer to consider the reality of America. It is true that we have launched our Bicentennial celebration without having achieved human perfection, but we have attained a very remarkable self-governed society that possesses the flexibility and the dynamism to grow and undertake an entirely new agenda, an agenda for America's third century.

So, I ask you to join me in helping to write that agenda. I am as determined as a President can be to seek national rediscovery of the belief in ourselves that characterized the most creative periods in our Nation's history. The greatest challenge of creativity, as I see it, lies ahead.

"EVIL EMPIRE" SPEECH

Ronald Reagan

1911–2004

40th President: January 20, 1981–January 20, 1989

When the hardliner Yuri Andropov came to power in the Soviet Union in November 1982, it seemed to herald a worsening of U.S.A.–U.S.S.R. relations. Certainly, the rhetoric from the American administration hardened still further: speaking to the National Association of Evangelicals, President Reagan took a moralistic and religious line in his criticism of the "Evil Empire."

The Soviets were unimpressed by the label: the Soviet press agency TASS said that it demonstrated that the Reagan administration could "think only in terms of confrontation and bellicose, lunatic anti-communism." Regan was to go on to negotiate important disarmament treaties with the Soviets.

A number of years ago, I heard a young father, a very prominent young man in the entertainment world, addressing a tremendous gathering in California. It was during the time of the cold war, and communism and our own way of life were very much on people's minds. And he was speaking to that subject. And suddenly, though, I heard him saying, "I love my little girls more than anything—" And I said to myself, "Oh, no, don't. You can't—don't say that." But I had underestimated him. He went on: "I would rather see my little girls die now, still believing in God, than have them grow up under communism and one day die no longer believing in God."

There were thousands of young people in that audience. They came to their feet with shouts of joy. They had instantly recognized the profound truth in what he had said, with regard to the physical and the soul and what was truly important.

Yes, let us pray for the salvation of all of those who live in that totalitarian darkness – pray they will discover the joy of knowing God. But until they do, let us be aware that while they preach the supremacy of the state, declare its omnipotence over individual man, and predict its eventual domination of all peoples on the Earth, they are the focus of evil in the modern world.

It was C. S. Lewis who, in his unforgettable "Screwtape Letters," wrote: "The greatest evil is not done now in those sordid 'dens of crime' that Dickens loved to paint. It is not even done in concentration camps and labor camps. In those we see its final result. But it is conceived and ordered (moved, seconded, carried and minuted) in clear, carpeted, warmed, and well-lighted offices, by quiet men with white collars and cut fingernails and smooth-shaven cheeks who do not need to raise their voice."

Well, because these "quiet men" do not "raise their voices," because they sometimes speak in soothing tones of brotherhood and peace, because, like other dictators before them, they're always making "their final territorial demand," some would have us accept them at their word and accommodate ourselves to their aggressive impulses. But if history teaches anything, it teaches that simple-minded appeasement or wishful thinking about our adversaries is folly. It means the betrayal of our past, the squandering of our freedom.

So, I urge you to speak out against those who would place the United States in a position of military and moral inferiority. You know, I've always believed that old Screwtape reserved his best efforts for those of you in the church. So, in your discussions of the nuclear freeze proposals, I urge you to beware the temptation of pride – the temptation of blithely declaring yourselves above it all and label both sides equally at fault, to ignore the facts of history and the aggressive impulses of an evil empire, to simply call the arms race a giant misunderstanding and thereby remove yourself from the struggle between right and wrong and good and evil.

REMARKS AT THE ANNUAL CONVENTION OF THE ANTI-DEFAMATION LEAGUE OF B'NAI B'RITH

Ronald Reagan

1911–2004
40th President: January 20, 1981–January 20, 1989

On June 10, 1983, President RonaldReagan addressed the Annual Convention of the Anti-Defamation League of B'nai B'rith – the Jewish organization dedicated to anti-racism and welfare issues, among many other things – over the telephone. At the time, Israeli forces occupied areas of Lebanon as a consequence of the 1982 war, and negotiations had concluded only the previous month that would allow these forces to withdraw to a security zone in the south of the country. Although this agreement was, in the end, never ratified, Israel completed the withdrawal of its forces to this zone in the south of Lebanon in 1985.

I know the Anti-Defamation League has justly earned the recognition as a champion of human rights. For seven decades, you've worked to ensure that all members of our society, no matter what their race, religion, or background, have an equal opportunity to succeed. And I deeply appreciate your support for my recent appointments to the U.S. Commission on Civil Rights. Like you, I, too, was deeply troubled by the strident attacks against them.

I know that we share a belief that all people, no matter where they live, have the right to freedom of religion. This is not a right that is any government's to give or to take away. It's our right from birth, because we're all children of God.

We believe it's our duty to defend freedom, not just here at home but everywhere people are persecuted for their beliefs. I was very disturbed that a Soviet spokesman said earlier this week the majority of Jews who want to be reunited with their families in Israel have left the Soviet Union. This official said that the portion of the 1.8 million Russian Jews who still want to leave have, and I quote, "Fallen victim to Zionist propaganda which brainwashes them.'

Well, as you know, the National Conference on Soviet Jewry estimates that by late 1979 at least 300,000 Jews had asked relatives abroad to send invitations needed for emigration. This was before the Soviets began blocking these invitations.

But in 1975, the Soviet Government signed the final act of the Helsinki Agreement. The Soviets pledged to deal in a positive and humanitarian spirit with the applications of persons who wish to be reunited with their families.

So, let us stand together, speak the truth, and tell the Soviets, stop persecuting innocent people. Let Israel's children go or face the world's condemnation for making a mockery of an historic agreement that was signed by 35 nations.

I'm delighted that Sam Lewis, our Ambassador to Israel, is with you today. I know that he'll be talking with you in greater detail about U.S. policies in the Middle East.

We're very pleased with the recent efforts of Secretary Shultz in working out the Israeli–Lebanon withdrawal agreement. This bold initiative by Israel and Lebanon is one more step toward a more stable Middle East. Our ultimate goal remains peace between Israel and all her Arab neighbors.

Only through peace can Israel achieve real security. But Israel cannot make peace alone. Other Arab states must formally recognize that Israel does exist and that she has a right to exist. We'll continue our diplomatic efforts to seek the withdrawal from Lebanon of all foreign forces, Syrian and PLO as well as Israeli. But we are very concerned about the Soviet buildup in Syria. I want you to know that we're committed to maintaining Israel's qualitative edge in the military balance of power. I have personally followed Israel's heroic struggle for survival ever since the founding of the State of Israel 35 years ago. As long as I'm President, the United States will be a rock of support. We will not waver in our commitment to protect Israel's security.

It's no coincidence that the same forces which are destabilizing the Middle East – the Soviet Union, Libya, the PLO – are also working hand in glove with Cuba to destabilize Central America. And I'd like to urge you to support this Nation's efforts to help our friends in Central America. This question isn't who has the most perfect democracy. The question is, who's trying to build democracy and who is determined to destroy it. Many nations, including the United States, which once condoned slavery, have evolved into better democracies over time. But nations which fall into the clutches of totalitarianism do not become free and democratic again. And freedom can't be lost in one nation without being diminished everywhere.

Again, as you embark on your next 70 years, you have the thanks of all Americans for a job well done and our best wishes for the future. May we continue to be allies, may God bless you, and may He be with us all in our human rights struggles ahead.

REMARKS ON EAST–WEST RELATIONS AT THE BRANDENBURG GATE IN WEST BERLIN

Ronald Reagan

1911–2004
40th President: January 20, 1981–January 20, 1989

As the Cold War thawed, the Reagan administration continued to take a hard line against the Soviet Union, providing military support to anti-communist armed movements in Afghanistan, Angola, and elsewhere. However, between 1985 and 1988, four summit meetings were held between President Ronald Reagan and the Soviet leader Mikhail Gorbachev. As relations theoretically improved, the American leadership constantly sought for ways to focus international pressure on Soviet policy, particularly regarding the U.S.S.R.'s client states in Eastern Europe.

The famous line "Mr. Gorbachev, tear down this wall!" was the subject of debate among Reagan's team before the speech was delivered. Detractors, including then Deputy National Security Advisor, Colin Powell, thought it was too confrontational. Nevertheless, Reagan decided to keep it in, and it has now become one of the most iconic sound bites of the Cold War era; when the wall began to be physically torn down by German protestors in November 1989, it began with hindsight to assume a prophetic significance.

We welcome change and openness; for we believe that freedom and security go together, that the advance of human liberty can only strengthen the cause of world peace. There is one sign the Soviets can make that would be unmistakable, that would advance dramatically the cause of freedom and peace. General Secretary Gorbachev, if you seek peace, if you seek prosperity for the Soviet Union and Eastern Europe, if you seek liberalization, come here to this gate. Mr. Gorbachev, open this gate. Mr. Gorbachev, tear down this wall!

TOWARD A NEW WORLD ORDER

George H. W. Bush

1924
41st President: January 20, 1989–January 20, 1993

On August 1, 1990, Iraqi forces invaded the country's southern neighbor Kuwait. Almost immediately, a coalition of more than thirty countries began making plans to liberate the oil-rich state and troops were deployed to Saudi Arabia and navies to the Persian Gulf. On September 11, President George H. W. Bush addressed a joint session of Congress on the invasion and the need for intervention for political and economic reasons, especially in the light of a perceived threat to Saudia Arabia. Congress authorized the invasion on January 12, 1991, and Operation Desert Storm began on January 17.

Mr. President and Mr. Speaker and Members of the United States Congress, distinguished guests, fellow Americans, thank you very much for that warm welcome. We gather tonight, witness to events in the Persian Gulf as significant as they are tragic. In the early morning hours of August 2, following negotiations and promises by Iraq's dictator Saddam Hussein not to use force, a powerful Iraqi army invaded its trusting and much weaker neighbor, Kuwait. Within 3 days, 120,000 Iraqi troops with 850 tanks had poured into Kuwait and moved south to threaten Saudi Arabia. It was then that I decided to act to check that aggression [...]

Our objectives in the Persian Gulf are clear, our goals defined and familiar: Iraq must withdraw from Kuwait completely, immediately, and without condition. Kuwait's legitimate government must be restored. The security and stability of the Persian Gulf must be assured. And American citizens abroad must be protected.

These goals are not ours alone. They've been endorsed by the United Nations Security Council five times in as many weeks. Most countries share our concern for principle. And many have a stake in the stability of the Persian Gulf. This is not, as Saddam Hussein would have it, the United States against Iraq. It is Iraq against the world [...]

We stand today at a unique and extraordinary moment. The crisis in the Persian Gulf, as grave as it is, also offers a rare opportunity to move toward an historic period of cooperation. Out of these troubled times, our fifth objective – a new world order – can emerge: a new era – freer from the threat of terror, stronger in the pursuit of justice, and more secure in the quest for peace. An era in which the nations of the world, East and West, North and South, can prosper and live in harmony. A hundred generations have searched for this elusive path to peace, while a thousand wars raged across the span of human endeavor. Today that new world is struggling to be born, a world quite different from the one we've known. A world where the rule of law supplants the rule of the jungle. A world in which nations recognize the shared responsibility for freedom and justice. A world where the strong respect the rights of the weak. This is the vision that I shared with President Gorbachev in Helsinki. He and other leaders from Europe, the Gulf, and around the world understand that how we manage this crisis today could shape the future for generations [...]

[...] America and the world must defend common vital interests – and we will. America and the world must support the rule of law – and we will. America and the world must stand up to aggression – and we will. And one thing more: In the pursuit of these goals America will not be intimidated.

Vital issues of principle are at stake. Saddam Hussein is literally trying to wipe a country off the face of the Earth. We do not exaggerate. Nor do we exaggerate when we say Saddam Hussein will fail. Vital economic interests are at risk as well. Iraq itself controls some 10 percent of the world's proven oil reserves. Iraq plus Kuwait controls twice that. An Iraq permitted to swallow Kuwait would have the economic and military power, as well as the arrogance, to intimidate and coerce its neighbors – neighbors who control the lion's share of the world's remaining oil reserves. We cannot permit a resource so vital to be dominated by one so ruthless. And we won't.

Recent events have surely proven that there is no substitute for American leadership. In the face of tyranny, let no one doubt American credibility and reliability. Let no one doubt our staying power. We will stand by our friends. One way or another, the leader of Iraq must learn this fundamental truth. From the outset, acting hand in hand with others, we've sought to fashion the broadest possible international response to Iraq's aggression. The level of world cooperation and condemnation of Iraq is unprecedented. Armed forces from countries spanning four continents are there at the request of King Fahd of Saudi Arabia to deter and, if need be, to defend against attack. Muslims and non-Muslims, Arabs and non-Arabs, soldiers from many nations stand shoulder to shoulder, resolute against Saddam Hussein's ambitions [...]

We're now in sight of a United Nations that performs as envisioned by its founders. We owe much to the outstanding leadership of Secretary-General Javier Perez de Cuellar. The United Nations is backing up its words with action. The Security Council has imposed mandatory economic sanctions on Iraq, designed to force Iraq to relinquish the spoils of its illegal conquest. The Security Council has also taken the decisive step of authorizing the use of all means necessary to ensure compliance with these sanctions. Together with our friends and allies, ships of the United States Navy are today patrolling Mideast waters. They've already intercepted more than 700 ships to enforce the sanctions. Three regional leaders I spoke with just yesterday told me that these sanctions are working. Iraq is feeling the heat. We continue to hope that Iraq's leaders will recalculate just what their aggression has cost them. They are cut off from world trade, unable to sell their oil. And only a tiny fraction of goods gets through [...]

I cannot predict just how long it will take to convince Iraq to withdraw from Kuwait. Sanctions will take time to have their full intended effect. We will continue to review all options with our allies, but let it be clear: we will not let this aggression stand.

Our interest, our involvement in the Gulf is not transitory. It predated Saddam Hussein's aggression and will survive it. Long after all our troops come home – and we all hope it's soon, very soon – there will be a lasting role for the United States in assisting the nations of the Persian Gulf. Our role then: to deter future aggression. Our role is to help our friends in their own self-defense. And something else: to curb the proliferation of chemical, biological, ballistic missile and, above all, nuclear technologies.

Let me also make clear that the United States has no quarrel with the Iraqi people. Our quarrel is with Iraq's dictator and with his aggression. Iraq will not be permitted to annex Kuwait. That's not a threat, that's not a boast, that's just the way it's going to be [...]

In the final analysis, our ability to meet our responsibilities abroad depends upon political will and consensus at home. This is never easy in democracies, for we govern only with the consent of the governed. And although free people in a free society are bound to have their differences, Americans traditionally come together in times of adversity and challenge.

Once again, Americans have stepped forward to share a tearful goodbye with their families before leaving for a strange and distant shore. At this very moment, they serve together with Arabs, Europeans, Asians, and Africans in defense of principle and the dream of a new world order. That's why they sweat and toil in the sand and the heat and the sun. If they can come together under such adversity, if old adversaries like the Soviet Union and the United States can work in common cause, then surely we who are so fortunate to be in this great Chamber – Democrats, Republicans, liberals, conservatives – can come together to fulfill our responsibilities here. Thank you. Good night. And God bless the United States of America.

ADDRESS TO CONGRESS AFTER 9/11

George W. Bush

1946
43rd President: January 20, 2001–January 20, 2009

Ten days after the 9/11 terrorist attacks on the Twin Towers of the World Trade Center in New York and the Pentagon in Washington and the failed attack using

United Airlines Flight 93 on either the Capitol or the White House, President George W. Bush addressed a joint session of Congress and the nation. He called on the Taliban regime of Afghanistan to surrender the al-Qaeda leadership, including Osama Bin Laden, or face invasion. The Taliban response was in the negative and troops were deployed the following month in Operation Enduring Freedom. The Taliban regime was overthrown, and although the country now has democratic institutions and a freely elected government, neither the Taliban nor al-Qaeda has ceased attacks and an international military force remains in place.

Mr. Speaker, Mr. President Pro Tempore, members of Congress, and fellow Americans, in the normal course of events, presidents come to this chamber to report on the state of the union. Tonight, no such report is needed; it has already been delivered by the American people...

We've seen the unfurling of flags, the lighting of candles, the giving of blood, the saying of prayers in English, Hebrew and Arabic.

We have seen the decency of a loving and giving people who have made the grief of strangers their own.

My fellow citizens, for the last nine days, the entire world has seen for itself the state of union, and it is strong.

Tonight, we are a country awakened to danger and called to defend freedom. Our grief has turned to anger and anger to resolution. Whether we bring our enemies to justice or bring justice to our enemies, justice will be done [...]

And on behalf of the American people, I thank the world for its outpouring of support [...]

On September the 11th, enemies of freedom committed an act of war against our country. Americans have known wars, but for the past 136 years they have been wars on foreign soil, except for one Sunday in 1941. Americans have known the casualties of war, but not at the center of a great city on a peaceful morning.

Americans have known surprise attacks, but never before on thousands of civilians.

All of this was brought upon us in a single day, and night fell on a different world, a world where freedom itself is under attack.

Americans have many questions tonight. Americans are asking, "Who attacked our country?"

The evidence we have gathered all points to a collection of loosely affiliated terrorist organizations known as al-Qaeda. They are some of the murderers indicted for bombing American embassies in Tanzania and Kenya and responsible for bombing the U.S.S. *Cole*.

Al-Qaeda is to terror what the Mafia is to crime. But its goal is not making money, its goal is remaking the world and imposing its radical beliefs on people everywhere [...]

By aiding and abetting murder, the Taliban regime is committing murder. And tonight the United States of America makes the following demands on the Taliban.

Deliver to United States authorities all of the leaders of al-Quaeda who hide in your land.

Release all foreign nationals, including American citizens you have unjustly imprisoned. Protect foreign journalists, diplomats and aid workers in your country. Close immediately and permanently every terrorist training camp in Afghanistan. And hand over every terrorist and every person and their support structure to appropriate authorities.

Give the United States full access to terrorist training camps, so we can make sure they are no longer operating.

These demands are not open to negotiation or discussion.

The Taliban must act and act immediately.

They will hand over the terrorists or they will share in their fate.
I also want to speak tonight directly to Muslims throughout the world. We respect your faith. It's practiced freely by many millions of Americans and by millions more in countries that America counts as friends. Its teachings are good and peaceful, and those who commit evil in the name of Allah blaspheme the name of Allah.

The terrorists are traitors to their own faith, trying, in effect, to hijack Islam itself.

The enemy of America is not our many Muslim friends. It is not our many Arab friends. Our enemy is a radical network of terrorists and every government that supports them.

Our war on terror begins with al-Qaeda, but it does not end there.
It will not end until every terrorist group of global reach has been found, stopped and defeated.

Americans are asking "Why do they hate us?"

They hate what they see right here in this chamber: a democratically elected government. Their leaders are self-appointed. They hate our freedoms: our freedom of religion, our freedom of speech, our freedom to vote and assemble and disagree with each other [...]

Americans are asking, "How will we fight and win this war?"

We will direct every resource at our command – every means of diplomacy, every tool of intelligence, every instrument of law enforcement, every financial influence, and every necessary weapon of war – to the destruction and to the defeat of the global terror network.

Now, this war will not be like the war against Iraq a decade ago, with a decisive liberation of territory and a swift conclusion. It will not look like the air war above Kosovo two years ago, where no ground troops were used and not a single American was lost in combat.

Our response involves far more than instant retaliation and isolated strikes.

Americans should not expect one battle, but a lengthy campaign unlike any other we have ever seen. It may include dramatic strikes visible on TV and covert operations secret even in success.

We will starve terrorists of funding, turn them one against another, drive them from place to place until there is no refuge or no rest.

And we will pursue nations that provide aid or safe haven to terrorism. Every nation in every region now has a decision to make: Either you are with us or you are with the terrorists.

From this day forward, any nation that continues to harbor or support terrorism will be regarded by the United States as a hostile regime. Our nation has been put on notice, we're not immune from attack. We will take defensive measures against terrorism to protect Americans [...]

This is not, however, just America's fight. And what is at stake is not just America's freedom.

This is the world's fight. This is civilization's fight. This is the fight of all who believe in progress and pluralism, tolerance and freedom.

We ask every nation to join us. We will ask and we will need the help of police forces, intelligence service and banking systems around the world. The United States is grateful that many nations and many international organizations have already responded with sympathy and with support – nations from Latin America to Asia to Africa to Europe to the Islamic world [...]

Americans are asking, "What is expected of us?"

I ask you to live your lives and hug your children.

I know many citizens have fears tonight, and I ask you to be calm and resolute, even in the face of a continuing threat.

I ask you to uphold the values of America and remember why so many have come here.

We're in a fight for our principles, and our first responsibility is to live by them. No one should be singled out for unfair treatment or unkind words because of their ethnic background or religious faith [...]

Great harm has been done to us. We have suffered great loss. And in our grief and anger we have found our mission and our moment.

Freedom and fear are at war. The advance of human freedom, the great achievement of our time and the great hope of every time, now depends on us.

Our nation, this generation, will lift the dark threat of violence from our people and our future. We will rally the world to this cause by our efforts, by our courage. We will not tire, we will not falter and we will not fail [...]

Even grief recedes with time and grace.

But our resolve must not pass. Each of us will remember what happened that day and to whom it happened. We will remember the moment the news came, where we were and what we were doing.

Some will remember an image of a fire or story or rescue. Some will carry memories of a face and a voice gone forever [...]

I will not forget the wound to our country and those who inflicted it. I will not yield, I will not rest, I will not relent in waging this struggle for freedom and security for the American people.

The course of this conflict is not known, yet its outcome is certain. Freedom and fear, justice and cruelty, have always been at war, and we know that God is not neutral between them.

Fellow citizens, we'll meet violence with patient justice, assured of the rightness of our cause and confident of the victories to come.

In all that lies before us, may God grant us wisdom and may he watch over the United States of America.

Thank you.

"MISSION ACCOMPLISHED" SPEECH

George W. Bush

1946
43rd President: January 20, 2001–January 20, 2009

Standing on the deck of U.S.S. Abraham Lincoln, in front of a banner proclaiming "Mission Accomplished," President George W. Bush addressed a crowd of military personnel. He started by saying that the major combat operations in Iraq were over and that work would now be directed toward reconstruction and the setting up of a new democratic government. He also repeated warnings that any terrorist who sought to harm America or its allies would bear the consequences. His assessment that operations in Iraq were by no means over and that insurgency would be a continuing problem have proved only too right, but the assertion that Saddam Hussein's regime was supporting al-Qaeda has since been discounted by most authorities.

[…] my fellow Americans, major combat operations in Iraq have ended. In the battle of Iraq, the United States and our allies have prevailed.
And now our coalition is engaged in securing and reconstructing that country.

In this battle, we have fought for the cause of liberty and for the peace of the world. Our nation and our coalition are proud of this accomplishment, yet it is you, the members of the United States military, who achieved it. Your courage, your willingness to face danger for your country and for each other made this day possible.

Because of you our nation is more secure. Because of you the tyrant has fallen and Iraq is free […]

This nation thanks all of the members of our coalition who joined in a noble cause. We thank the armed forces of the United Kingdom, Australia and Poland who shared in the hardships of war. We thank all of the citizens of Iraq who welcomed our troops and joined in the liberation of their own country.

And tonight, I have a special word for Secretary Rumsfeld, for General Franks and for all the men and women who wear the uniform of the United States: America is grateful for a job well done.

With new tactics and precision weapons, we can achieve military objectives without directing violence against civilians.

No device of man can remove the tragedy from war, yet it is a great advance when the guilty have far more to fear from war than the innocent.

In the images of celebrating Iraqis we have also seen the ageless appeal of human freedom. Decades of lies and intimidation could not make the Iraqi people love their oppressors or desire their own enslavement.

Men and women in every culture need liberty like they need food and water and air. Everywhere that freedom arrives, humanity rejoices and everywhere that freedom stirs, let tyrants fear.

We have difficult work to do in Iraq. We're bringing order to parts of that country that remain dangerous. We're pursuing and finding leaders of the old regime who will be held to account for their crimes. We've begun the search for hidden chemical and biological weapons, and already know of hundreds of sites that will be investigated [...]

The transition from dictatorship to democracy will take time, but it is worth every effort. Our coalition will stay until our work is done and then we will leave and we will leave behind a free Iraq.

The battle of Iraq is one victory in a war on terror that began on September the 11th, 2001 and still goes on [...]

The liberation of Iraq is a crucial advance in the campaign against terror. We have removed an ally of al-Qaeda and cut off a source of terrorist funding [...]

And wherever you go, you carry a message of hope, a message that is ancient and ever new. In the words of the prophet Isaiah, "To the captives, come out; and to those in darkness, be free."

Thank you for serving our country and our cause.

May God bless you all. And may God continue to bless America.

"A MORE PERFECT UNION" SPEECH

Barack Obama

1961
44th President: January 20, 2009–January 20, 2017

It was inevitable that America's first black president would have to comment on his origins, particularly prior to his election. This speech was given in the course of Barack Obama's campaign for the Democratic presidential nomination, and touched on difficult topics such as black "anger" and white "resentment." The speech's title is taken from the Preamble to the U.S. Constitution, and closed with a plea for America to move beyond "racial stalemate."

The New York Times *called the speech a "Profile in Courage," and after the election, The* New Yorker *credited it as one of the critical factors that won Obama the presidential election.*

I'm the son of a black man from Kenya and a white woman from Kansas. I was raised with the help of a white grandfather who survived a Depression to serve in Patton's army during World War II, and a white grandmother who worked on a bomber assembly line at Fort Leavenworth while he was overseas. I've gone to some of the best schools in America and I've lived in one of the world's poorest nations. I am married to a black American who carries within her the blood of slaves and slave owners, an inheritance we pass on to our two precious daughters. I have brothers, sisters, nieces, nephews, uncles, and cousins of every race and every hue scattered across three continents. And for as long as I live, I will never forget that in no other country on earth is my story even possible. It's a story that hasn't made me the most conventional of candidates. But it is a story that has seared into my genetic makeup the idea that this nation is more than the sum of its parts – that out of many, we are truly one.

REMARKS TO THE TURKISH PARLIAMENT

Barack Obama

1961
44th President: January 20, 2009–January 20, 2017

If America's relationship with the communist powers was the key issue of twentieth-century foreign policy, it seems that relations with the Islamic countries, and Islam at home, are coming to define the policies of the twenty-first. On a two-day visit to Turkey in 2009, President Barack Obama took a conciliatory approach, with rhetoric of "building bridges" and "coming together." The speech opened with criticism of the U.S.'s domestic handling of racial history, which contrasted with previous presidents' frequent emphasis on America's singular moral rightness, and concentrated on conciliation and co-operation between the Islamic and Western worlds.

I know there have been difficulties these last few years. I know that the trust that binds the United States and Turkey has been strained, and I know that strain is shared in many places where the Muslim faith is practiced. So let me say this as clearly as I can: The United States is not, and will never be, at war with Islam. [Applause.] In fact, our partnership with the Muslim world is critical not just in rolling back the violent ideologies that people of all faiths reject, but also to strengthen opportunity for all its people.

I also want to be clear that America's relationship with the Muslim community, the Muslim world, cannot, and will not, just be based upon opposition to terrorism. We seek broader engagement based on mutual interest and mutual respect. We will listen carefully, we will bridge misunderstandings, and we will seek common ground. We will be respectful, even when we do not agree. We will convey our deep appreciation for the Islamic faith, which has done so much over the centuries to shape the world – including in my own country. The United States has been enriched by Muslim Americans. Many other Americans have Muslims in their families or have lived in a Muslim-majority country – I know, because I am one of them.

Above all, above all we will demonstrate through actions our commitment to a better future. I want to help more children get the education that they need to succeed. We want to promote health care in places where people are vulnerable. We want to expand the trade and investment that can bring prosperity for all people. In the months ahead, I will present specific programs to advance these goals. Our focus will be on what we can do, in partnership with people across the Muslim world, to advance our common hopes and our common dreams. And when people look back on this time, let it be said of America that we extended the hand of friendship to all people.

There's an old Turkish proverb: "You cannot put out fire with flames." America knows this. Turkey knows this. There's some who must be met by force, they will not compromise. But force alone cannot solve our problems, and it is no alternative to extremism. The future must belong to those who create, not those who destroy.

That is the future we must work for, and we must work for it together.

INAUGURAL ADDRESSES

---≈---

John Adams

---•---

1735–1826
2nd President: March 4, 1797–March 4, 1801

*When George Washington declined to stand for a third term, the United States had
its first contested presidential election, of which John Adams was the winner. Anxious
to build on the foundation laid by his illustrious predecessor, in his inauguration
speech, Adams heavily emphasized the young nation's vitality and growth, and
the importance of continuing what had been started. Always high-strung, he said
afterwards that the inauguration ceremony made him feel as if he was playing a part:
"the most affecting and overpowering scene I ever acted in."*

The operation of [the Constitution] has equaled the most sanguine expectations of
its friends, and from an habitual attention to it, satisfaction in its administration,
and delight in its effects upon the peace, order, prosperity, and happiness of the
nation I have acquired an habitual attachment to it and veneration for it.
What other form of government, indeed, can so well deserve our esteem and love?
There may be little solidity in an ancient idea that congregations of men into cities
and nations are the most pleasing objects in the sight of superior intelligences, but
this is very certain, that to a benevolent human mind there can be no spectacle
presented by any nation more pleasing, more noble, majestic, or august, than an
assembly like that which has so often been seen in this and the other Chamber of
Congress, of a Government in which the Executive authority, as well as that of all
the branches of the Legislature, are exercised by citizens selected at regular periods
by their neighbors to make and execute laws for the general good. Can anything
essential, anything more than mere ornament and decoration, be added to this

by robes and diamonds? Can authority be more amiable and respectable when it descends from accidents or institutions established in remote antiquity than when it springs fresh from the hearts and judgments of an honest and enlightened people? For it is the people only that are represented. It is their power and majesty that is reflected, and only for their good, in every legitimate government, under whatever form it may appear. The existence of such a government as ours for any length of time is a full proof of a general dissemination of knowledge and virtue throughout the whole body of the people. And what object or consideration more pleasing than this can be presented to the human mind? If national pride is ever justifiable or excusable it is when it springs, not from power or riches, grandeur or glory, but from conviction of national innocence, information, and benevolence.

Thomas Jefferson

1743–1826
3rd President: March 4, 1801–March 4, 1809

After the very closely fought presidential election of 1800, Thomas Jefferson was declared the winner only in late February 1801. In his inaugural address, 25 years after he had drafted the Declaration of Independence, he set out his vision for the future of America, with low taxes, as little interference from the U.S. Government in people's daily lives as possible, equal justice for all, and peaceful relations with other nations. His gratitude that a wide ocean separated the U.S.A. from the squabbling countries of Europe formed a cornerstone of his foreign policy: the non-interference that lasted for generations and presaged the Monroe Doctrine.

Called upon to undertake the duties of the first executive office of our country, I avail myself of the presence of that portion of my fellow citizens which is here assembled to express my grateful thanks for the favor with which they have been pleased to look toward me, to declare a sincere consciousness that the task is above my talents, and that I approach it with those anxious and awful presentiments which the greatness of the charge and the weakness of my powers so justly inspire.

A rising nation, spread over a wide and fruitful land, traversing all the seas with the rich productions of their industry, engaged in commerce with nations who feel power and forget right, advancing rapidly to destinies beyond the reach of mortal eye – when I contemplate these transcendent objects, and see the honor, the happiness, and the hopes of this beloved country committed to the issue, and the auspices of this day, I shrink from the contemplation, and humble myself before the magnitude of the undertaking. Utterly, indeed, should I despair did not the presence of many whom I here see remind me that in the other high authorities provided by our Constitution I shall find resources of wisdom, of virtue, and of zeal on which to rely under all difficulties […]

Let us, then, with courage and confidence pursue our own Federal and Republican principles, our attachment to union and representative government. Kindly separated by nature and a wide ocean from the exterminating havoc of one quarter of the globe; too high-minded to endure the degradations of the others; possessing a chosen country, with room enough for our descendants to the thousandth and thousandth generation; entertaining a due sense of our equal right to the use of our own faculties, to the acquisitions of our own industry, to honor and confidence from our fellow-citizens, resulting not from birth, but from our actions and their sense of them; enlightened by a benign religion, professed, indeed, and practiced in various forms, yet all of them inculcating honesty, truth, temperance, gratitude, and the love of man; acknowledging and adoring an overruling Providence, which by all its dispensations proves that it delights in the happiness of man here and his greater happiness hereafter – with all these blessings, what more is necessary to make us a happy and a prosperous people? Still one thing more, fellow-citizens – a wise and frugal Government, which shall restrain men from injuring one another, shall leave them otherwise free to regulate their own pursuits of industry and improvement, and shall not take from the mouth of labor the bread it has earned […]

About to enter, fellow-citizens, on the exercise of duties which comprehend everything dear and valuable to you, it is proper you should understand what I deem the essential principles of our Government, and consequently those which ought to shape its Administration. I will compress them within the narrowest compass they will bear, stating the general principle, but not all its limitations. Equal and exact justice to all men, of whatever state or persuasion, religious or political; peace, commerce, and honest friendship with all nations, entangling alliances with none; the support of the State governments in all their rights, as the most competent administrations for our domestic concerns and the surest bulwarks against antirepublican tendencies; the preservation of the General Government in its whole constitutional vigour, as the sheet anchor of our peace at home and safety abroad; a jealous care of the right of election by the people – a mild and safe corrective of abuses which are lopped by the sword of revolution where peaceable remedies are unprovided; absolute acquiescence in the decisions of the majority, the vital principle of republics, from which is no appeal but to force, the vital principle and immediate parent of despotism; a well disciplined militia, our best reliance in peace and for the first moments of war, till regulars may relieve them; the supremacy of the civil over the military authority; economy in the public expense, that labor may be lightly burthened; the honest payment of our debts and sacred preservation of the public faith; encouragement of agriculture, and of commerce as its handmaid; the diffusion of information and arraignment of all abuses at the bar of the public reason; freedom of religion; freedom of the press, and freedom of person under the protection of the habeas corpus, and trial by juries impartially selected. These principles form the bright constellation which has gone before us and guided our steps through an age of revolution and reformation. The wisdom of our sages and blood of our heroes have been devoted to their attainment. They should be the creed of our political faith, the text of civic instruction, the touchstone by which to try the services of those we trust; and should we wander from them in moments of error or of alarm, let us hasten to retrace our steps and to regain the road which alone leads to peace, liberty, and safety [...]

Relying, then, on the patronage of your good will, I advance with obedience to the work, ready to retire from it whenever you become sensible how much better choice it is in your power to make. And may that Infinite Power which rules the destinies of the universe lead our councils to what is best, and give them a favorable issue for your peace and prosperity.

Martin van Buren

1782–1862
8th President: March 4, 1837–March 4, 1841

Standing at five foot six inches, Martin van Buren was known as the "Little Magician," and elected at a time of prosperity; one that was soon to be punctured by the financial panic of 1837. At the time of his inauguration, van Buren commented on the rapid expansion of the United States, and its likely dangers in terms of the over-stretching of resources and governmental systems. During his time in office, he blocked the annexation of the Republic of Texas, both to avoid adding additional slave-owning territory to the U.S.A. and for fear of the war with Mexico that a shared border was likely to bring.

Certain danger was foretold from the extension of our territory, the multiplication of States, and the increase of population. Our system was supposed to be adapted only to boundaries comparatively narrow. These have been widened beyond conjecture; the members of our Confederacy are already doubled, and the numbers of our people are incredibly augmented.

William Henry Harrison

1773–1841
9th President: March 4, 1841–April 4, 1841

William Henry Harrison holds two notable records: the shortest presidency in American history and the longest inaugural address. The address took an hour and forty-five minutes, and was delivered by a coatless Harrison in a howling snowstorm.

Later that day, he was taken ill with a cold that turned into pneumonia and led to his death a month later. The speech that both launched and effectively ended a presidency is largely unremarkable, but Harrison did leave us this accurate observation about the changeless (bad) behavior of governments over the centuries.

It was the remark of a Roman consul in an early period of that celebrated Republic that a most striking contrast was observable in the conduct of candidates for offices of power and trust before and after obtaining them, they seldom carrying out in the latter case the pledges and promises made in the former. However much the world may have improved in many respects in the lapse of upward of two thousand years since the remark was made by the virtuous and indignant Roman, I fear that a strict examination of the annals of some of the modern elective governments would develop similar instances of violated confidence.

James K. Polk

1795–1849
11th President: March 4, 1845–March 4, 1849

James K. Polk presided over a period of great expansion for the U.S.A., before the devastations and disillusionments of the Civil War. One of the most notable events of his presidency was the annexation of Texas, on December 29, 1845. However, this was to lead to war with Mexico on the newly-created U.S.–Mexico border in 1846–1848 – which the U.S. won conclusively. Polk also threatened war with the U.K over control of the then known Oregon County, though the dispute was settled peacefully.

The inestimable value of our Federal Union is felt and acknowledged by all. By this system of united and confederated States our people are permitted collectively and individually to seek their own happiness in their own way, and the consequences have been most auspicious. Since the Union was formed the number of the States has increased from thirteen to twenty-eight; two of these have taken their position as members of the Confederacy within the last week. Our population has increased from three to twenty millions. New communities and States are seeking protection under its aegis, and multitudes from the Old World are flocking to our shores to participate in its blessings. Beneath its benign sway peace and prosperity prevail. Freed from the burdens and miseries of war, our trade and intercourse have extended throughout the world. Mind, no longer tasked in devising means to accomplish or resist schemes of ambition, usurpation, or conquest, is devoting itself to man's true interests in developing his faculties and powers and the capacity of nature to minister to his enjoyments. Genius is free to announce its inventions and discoveries, and the hand is free to accomplish whatever the head conceives not incompatible with the rights of a fellow-being. All distinctions of birth or of rank have been abolished. All citizens, whether native or adopted, are placed upon terms of precise equality. All are entitled to equal rights and equal protection. No union exists between church and state, and perfect freedom of opinion is guaranteed to all sects and creeds.

These are some of the blessings secured to our happy land by our Federal Union. To perpetuate them it is our sacred duty to preserve it.

Zachary Taylor

1784–1850
12th President: March 4, 1849–July 9, 1850

Zachary Taylor spent only sixteen months in office before dying of a stomach ailment. He did not have much experience of foreign policy when he became president, but he was conscious of the desirability of negotiations over further war, particularly with Britain. In the Clayton–Bulwer Treaty, Taylor's last act of state, both countries agreed to renounce control over a proposed canal to be built across Nicaragua. This tentative step moved the U.S. and U.K. toward the friendly alliance that emerged in the second half of the nineteenth century, and that endures today.

As American freemen we can not but sympathize in all efforts to extend the blessings of civil and political liberty, but at the same time we are warned by the admonitions of history and the voice of our own beloved Washington to abstain from entangling alliances with foreign nations. In all disputes between conflicting governments it is our interest not less than our duty to remain strictly neutral, while our geographical position, the genius of our institutions and our people, the advancing spirit of civilization, and, above all, the dictates of religion direct us to the cultivation of peaceful and friendly relations with all other powers. It is to be hoped that no international question can now arise which a government confident in its own strength and resolved to protect its own just rights may not settle by wise negotiation; and it eminently becomes a government like our own, founded on the morality and intelligence of its citizens and upheld by their affections, to exhaust every resort of honorable diplomacy before appealing to arms. In the conduct of our foreign relations I shall conform to these views, as I believe them essential to the best interests and the true honor of the country.

James Buchanan

1791–1868
15th President: March 4, 1857–March 4, 1861

The inauguration of James Buchanan is considered more notable for its culinary extravagance – a 1997 New York Times *article calculated that about $3,000 dollars (over $80,000 in today's money) was spent on the wine alone – than for its effect on history. His presidency was noted for its failure to address the growing divide* *between pro- and anti-slavery camps that would eventually lead to the Civil War. Buchanan could turn out high sentiments on morality as well as the next statesman, although it could not protect him from posterity's label of "Worst President," consistently coming bottom of popular polls.*

Next in importance to the maintenance of the Constitution and the Union is the duty of preserving the Government free from the taint or even the suspicion of corruption. Public virtue is the vital spirit of republics, and history proves that when this has decayed and the love of money has usurped its place […] the substance has departed forever.

Abraham Lincoln

1809–1865
16th President: 4 March 1861–15 April 1865

Lincoln's second inaugural address came at a time when the Civil War was still in progress but the imminent victory of the Union was clear: Confederate forces were to surrender just a month later, on April 9. Lincoln himself was to outlive the war by just five days, as he was assassinated on 14 April.

Sealing his reputation as a great statesman, Lincoln took a pragmatic approach to Reconstruction – the reordering and regeneration of the defeated South – and the healing of the souls of the nation. However, to quote Lincoln himself, the speech was "not immediately popular," thanks to his blunt description of the conflict as the "woe due" to the entire nation, inflicted by God as punishment for the evil of slavery. "Men are not flattered by being shown that there has been a difference of purpose between the Almighty and them," he wrote in a letter to newspaper publisher Thurlow Weed. The final paragraph of the speech is often-quoted as a preeminent example of a great president setting his country's face to the future after a terrible crisis.

At this second appearing to take the oath of the presidential office there is less occasion for an extended address than there was at the first. Then a statement, somewhat in detail, of a course to be pursued seemed fitting and proper. Now, at the expiration of four years, during which public declarations have been constantly called forth on every point and phase of the great contest which still absorbs the attention and engrosses the energies of the nation, little that is new could be presented. The progress of our arms, upon which all else chiefly depends, is as well known to the public as to myself, and it is, I trust, reasonably satisfactory and encouraging to all. With high hope for the future, no prediction in regard to it is ventured.

On the occasion corresponding to this four years ago all thoughts were anxiously directed to an impending civil war. All dreaded it; all sought to avert it. While the inaugural address was being delivered from this place, devoted altogether to saving the Union without war, insurgent agents were in the city seeking to destroy it without war – seeking to dissolve the Union and divide effects by negotiation. Both parties deprecated war, but one of them would make war rather than let the nation survive, and the other would accept war rather than let it perish, and the war came. One-eighth of the whole population were colored slaves, not distributed generally over the Union, but localized in the southern part of it. These slaves constituted a peculiar and powerful interest. All knew that this interest was somehow the cause of war. To strengthen, perpetuate, and extend this interest was the object for which the insurgents would rend the Union even by war, while the Government claimed no right to do more than to restrict the territorial enlargement of it. Neither party expected for the war the magnitude or the duration which it has already attained. Neither anticipated that the cause of the conflict might cease with or even before the conflict itself should cease. Each looked for an easier triumph, and a result less fundamental and astounding. Both read the same Bible and pray to the same God, and each invokes His aid against the other. It may seem strange that any men should dare to ask a just God's assistance in wringing their bread from the sweat of other men's faces, but let us judge not, that we be not judged. The prayers of both could not be answered. That of neither has been answered fully. The Almighty has His own purposes. "Woe unto the world because of offenses; for it must needs be that offenses come, but woe to that man by whom the offense cometh." If we shall suppose that American slavery is one of those offenses which, in the providence of God, must needs come, but which, having continued through His appointed time, He now wills to remove, and that He gives to both North and South this terrible war as the woe due to those by whom the offense came, shall we discern therein any departure from those divine attributes which the believers in a living God always ascribe to Him? Fondly do we hope, fervently do we pray, that this mighty scourge of war may speedily pass away. Yet, if God wills that it continue until all the wealth piled by the bondsman's two hundred and fifty years of unrequited toil shall be sunk, and until every drop of blood drawn with the lash shall be paid by another drawn with the sword, as was said three thousand years ago, so still it must be said "the judgments of the Lord are true and righteous altogether."

With malice toward none, with charity for all, with firmness in the right as God gives us to see the right, let us strive on to finish the work we are in, to bind up the nation's wounds, to care for him who shall have borne the battle and for his widow and his orphan, to do all which may achieve and cherish a just and lasting peace among ourselves and with all nations.

Grover Cleveland

1837–1908
22nd President: March 4, 1885–March 4, 1889
24th President: March 4, 1893–March 4, 1897

The first Democrat to be elected to the presidency since 1856, Grover Cleveland benefited from the Republicans' candidate, James Blaine, who alienated many members of the GOP. His inspiring inaugural address called for "non-sectional" co-operation – after a notoriously spiteful campaign – promised a continuation of the foreign policies of not getting embroiled in other countries' disputes but protecting U.S. interests against any threats, and a replacement of incompetent time-serving public employees with what could be called "a government of all the talents."

In the presence of this vast assemblage of my countrymen I am about to supplement and seal by the oath which I shall take the manifestation of the will of a great and free people. In the exercise of their power and right of self-government they have committed to one of their fellow-citizens a supreme and sacred trust, and he here consecrates himself to their service [...]

Today the executive branch of the Government is transferred to new keeping. But this is still the Government of all the people, and it should be none the less an object of their affectionate solicitude [...] Moreover, if from this hour we cheerfully and honestly abandon all sectional prejudice and distrust, and determine, with manly confidence in one another, to work out harmoniously the achievements of our national destiny, we shall deserve to realize all the benefits which our happy form of government can bestow [...]

By the Father of his Country our Constitution was commended for adoption as "the result of a spirit of amity and mutual concession." In that same spirit it should be administered, in order to promote the lasting welfare of the country and to secure the full measure of its priceless benefits to us and to those who will succeed to the blessings of our national life. The large variety of diverse and competing interests subject to Federal control, persistently seeking the recognition of their claims, need give us no fear that "the greatest good to the greatest number" will fail to be accomplished if in the halls of national legislation that spirit of amity and mutual concession shall prevail in which the Constitution had its birth. If this involves the surrender or postponement of private interests and the abandonment of local advantages, compensation will be found in the assurance that the common interest is subserved and the general welfare advanced.

In the discharge of my official duty I shall endeavor to be guided by a just and unstrained construction of the Constitution, a careful observance of the distinction between the powers granted to the Federal Government and those reserved to the States or to the people, and by a cautious appreciation of those functions which by the Constitution and laws have been especially assigned to the executive branch of the government.

But he who takes the oath today to preserve, protect, and defend the Constitution of the United States only assumes the solemn obligation which every patriotic citizen – on the farm, in the workshop, in the busy marts of trade, and everywhere – should share with him. The Constitution which prescribes his oath, my countrymen, is yours; the government you have chosen him to administer for a time is yours; the suffrage which executes the will of freemen is yours; the laws and the entire scheme of our civil rule, from the town meeting to the State capitals and the national capital, is yours. Your every voter, as surely as your Chief Magistrate, under the same high sanction, though in a different sphere, exercises a public trust. Nor is this all. Every citizen owes to the country a vigilant watch and close scrutiny of its public servants and a fair and reasonable estimate of their fidelity and usefulness. Thus is the people's will impressed upon the whole framework of our civil polity – municipal, State, and Federal [...]

The genius of our institutions, the needs of our people in their home life, and the attention which is demanded for the settlement and development of the resources of our vast territory dictate the scrupulous avoidance of any departure from that foreign policy commended by the history, the traditions, and the prosperity of our Republic. It is the policy of independence, favored by our position and defended by our known love of justice and by our power. It is the policy of peace suitable to our interests. It is the policy of neutrality, rejecting any share in foreign broils and ambitions upon other continents and repelling their intrusion here. It is the policy of Monroe and of Washington and Jefferson – "Peace, commerce, and honest friendship with all nations; entangling alliance with none." [...]

The conscience of the people demands that the Indians within our boundaries shall be fairly and honestly treated as wards of the Government and their education and civilization promoted with a view to their ultimate citizenship, and that polygamy in the Territories, destructive of the family relation and offensive to the moral sense of the civilized world, shall be repressed [...]

The people demand reform in the administration of the government and the application of business principles to public affairs. As a means to this end, civil-service reform should be in good faith enforced. Our citizens have the right to protection from the incompetency of public employees who hold their places solely as the reward of partisan service, and from the corrupting influence of those who promise and the vicious methods of those who expect such rewards; and those who worthily seek public employment have the right to insist that merit and competency shall be recognized instead of party subserviency or the surrender of honest political belief [...]

These topics and the constant and ever-varying wants of an active and enterprising population may well receive the attention and the patriotic endeavor of all who make and execute the Federal law. Our duties are practical and call for industrious application, an intelligent perception of the claims of public office, and, above all, a firm determination, by united action, to secure to all the people of the land the full benefits of the best form of government ever vouchsafed to man. And let us not trust to human effort alone, but humbly acknowledging the power and goodness of Almighty God, who presides over the destiny of nations, and who has at all times been revealed in our country's history, let us invoke His aid and His blessings upon our labors.

Warren G. Harding

1865–1923
29th President: March 4, 1921–August 2, 1923

At the first presidential inauguration after World War I, Warren Harding set out his philosophy and major aims for his term, including the God-given righteousness of the American Republic, continuation of the previous policy of non-involvement in other countries' business or wars unless not to do so would be detrimental to the U.S.A., mediation and conciliation with former enemies, reduced taxation when possible, economic recovery, the continuation of import tariffs to protect U.S. manufacturing, reconstruction, improvement of welfare through the creation of wealth, the need for unselfishness, the possibility of a universal "draft" for civil or military service, and an outlawing of profiteering. He died just two-and-a-half years into his presidency.

When one surveys the world about him after the great storm, noting the marks of destruction and yet rejoicing in the ruggedness of the things which withstood it, if he is an American he breathes the clarified atmosphere with a strange mingling of regret and new hope. We have seen a world passion spend its fury, but we contemplate our Republic unshaken, and hold our civilization secure. Liberty – liberty within the law – and civilization are inseparable, and though both were threatened we find them now secure; and there comes to Americans the profound assurance that our representative government is the highest expression and surest guaranty of both [...]

The recorded progress of our Republic, materially and spiritually, in itself proves the wisdom of the inherited policy of noninvolvement in Old World affairs.

Confident of our ability to work out our own destiny, and jealously guarding our right to do so, we seek no part in directing the destinies of the Old World. We do not mean to be entangled. We will accept no responsibility except as our own conscience and judgment, in each instance, may determine.

Our eyes never will be blind to a developing menace, our ears never deaf to the call of civilization. We recognize the new order in the world, with the closer contacts which progress has wrought. We sense the call of the human heart for fellowship, fraternity, and cooperation. We crave friendship and harbor no hate. But America, our America, the America builded on the foundation laid by the inspired fathers, can be a party to no permanent military alliance. It can enter into no political commitments, nor assume any economic obligations which will subject our decisions to any other than our own authority [...]

The success of our popular government rests wholly upon the correct interpretation of the deliberate, intelligent, dependable popular will of America. In a deliberate questioning of a suggested change of national policy, where internationality was to supersede nationality, we turned to a referendum, to the American people. There was ample discussion, and there is a public mandate in manifest understanding. America is ready to encourage, eager to initiate, anxious to participate in any seemly program likely to lessen the probability of war, and promote that brotherhood of mankind which must be God's highest conception of human relationship. Because we cherish ideals of justice and peace, because we appraise international comity and helpful relationship no less highly than any people of the world, we aspire to a high place in the moral leadership of civilization, and we hold a maintained America, the proven Republic, the unshaken temple of representative democracy, to be not only an inspiration and example, but the highest agency of strengthening good will and promoting accord on both continents [...] We must understand that ties of trade bind nations in closest intimacy, and none may receive except as he gives. We have not strengthened ours in accordance with our resources or our genius, notably on our own continent, where a galaxy of republics reflects the glory of new-world democracy, but in the new order of finance and trade we mean to promote enlarged activities and seek expanded confidence [...]

Amid it all we have riveted the gaze of all civilization to the unselfishness and the righteousness of representative democracy, where our freedom never has made offensive warfare, never has sought territorial aggrandizement through force, never has turned to the arbitrament of arms until reason has been exhausted. When the governments of the earth shall have established a freedom like our own and shall have sanctioned the pursuit of peace as we have practiced it, I believe the last sorrow and the final sacrifice of international warfare will have been written.

Let me speak to the maimed and wounded soldiers who are present today, and through them convey to their comrades the gratitude of the Republic for their sacrifices in its defense. A generous country will never forget the services you rendered, and you may hope for a policy under government that will relieve any maimed successors from taking your places on another such occasion as this [...]

Out of such universal service will come a new unity of spirit and purpose, a new confidence and consecration, which would make our defense impregnable, our triumph assured. Then we should have little or no disorganization of our economic, industrial, and commercial systems at home, no staggering war debts, no swollen fortunes to flout the sacrifices of our soldiers, no excuse for sedition, no pitiable slackerism, no outrage of treason. Envy and jealousy would have no soil for their menacing development, and revolution would be without the passion which engenders it [...]

The business world reflects the disturbance of war's reaction. Herein flows the lifeblood of material existence. The economic mechanism is intricate and its parts interdependent, and has suffered the shocks and jars incident to abnormal demands, credit inflations, and price upheavals. The normal balances have been impaired, the channels of distribution have been clogged, the relations of labor and management have been strained. We must seek the readjustment with care and courage. Our people must give and take. Prices must reflect the receding fever of war activities. Perhaps we never shall know the old levels of wages again, because war invariably readjusts compensations, and the necessaries of life will show their inseparable relationship, but we must strive for normalcy to reach stability. All the penalties will not be light, nor evenly distributed. There is no way of making them so. There is no instant step from disorder to order. We must face a condition of grim reality, charge off our losses and start afresh. It is the oldest lesson of civilization. I would like government to do all it can to mitigate; then, in understanding, in mutuality of interest, in concern for the common good, our tasks will be solved. No altered system will work a miracle. Any wild experiment will only add to the confusion. Our best assurance lies in efficient administration of our proven system [...]

I speak for administrative efficiency, for lightened tax burdens, for sound commercial practices, for adequate credit facilities, for sympathetic concern for all agricultural problems, for the omission of unnecessary interference of Government with business, for an end to Government's experiment in business, and for more efficient business in Government administration. With all of this must attend a mindfulness of the human side of all activities, so that social, industrial, and economic justice will be squared with the purposes of a righteous people.

With the nationwide induction of womanhood into our political life, we may count upon her intuitions, her refinements, her intelligence, and her influence to exalt the social order. We count upon her exercise of the full privileges and the performance of the duties of citizenship to speed the attainment of the highest state.

I wish for an America no less alert in guarding against dangers from within than it is watchful against enemies from without. Our fundamental law recognizes no class, no group, no section; there must be none in legislation or administration.

The supreme inspiration is the common weal. Humanity hungers for international peace, and we crave it with all mankind. My most reverent prayer for America is for industrial peace, with its rewards, widely and generally distributed, amid the inspirations of equal opportunity. No one justly may deny the equality of opportunity which made us what we are. We have mistaken unpreparedness to embrace it to be a challenge of the reality, and due concern for making all citizens fit for participation will give added strength of citizenship and magnify our achievement […]

Service is the supreme commitment of life. I would rejoice to acclaim the era of the Golden Rule and crown it with the autocracy of service. I pledge an administration wherein all the agencies of government are called to serve, and ever promote an understanding of government purely as an expression of the popular will […]

I accept my part with single-mindedness of purpose and humility of spirit, and implore the favor and guidance of God in His Heaven. With these I am unafraid, and confidently face the future.

I have taken the solemn oath of office on that passage of Holy Writ wherein it is asked: "What doth the Lord require but to do justly, and to love mercy, and to walk humbly with thy God?' This I plight to God and country.

Franklin D. Roosevelt

1882–1945
32nd President: March 4, 1933–April 12, 1945

In 1933, America was in the depths of the Great Depression that had followed the Wall Street Crash of 1929. FDR formulated a detailed plan to revitalize the U.S. economy, help the urban and rural poor and the unemployed, whilst also reforming the financial institutions whose irresponsibility had caused the mess. This plan was known as the New Deal. In his first inaugural address in March 1933, Roosevelt laid the blame at the feet of financiers, profit-seeking, and capitalism's overwhelming self-interest, sentiments echoed in another inaugural address almost 76 years later.

This is a day of national consecration. And I am certain that on this day my fellow Americans expect that on my induction into the Presidency, I will address them with a candour and a decision which the present situation of our people impels.

This is preeminently the time to speak the truth, the whole truth, frankly and boldly. Nor need we shrink from honestly facing conditions in our country today. This great Nation will endure, as it has endured, will revive and will prosper.

So, first of all, let me assert my firm belief that the only thing we have to fear is fear itself – nameless, unreasoning, unjustified terror which paralyzes needed efforts to convert retreat into advance. In every dark hour of our national life, a leadership of frankness and of vigor has met with that understanding and support of the people themselves which is essential to victory. And I am convinced that you will again give that support to leadership in these critical days [...]

[...] The rulers of the exchange of mankind's goods have failed, through their own stubbornness and their own incompetence, have admitted their failure, and have abdicated. Practices of the unscrupulous money changers stand indicted in the court of public opinion, rejected by the hearts and minds of men [...]

Yes, the money changers have fled from their high seats in the temple of our civilization. We may now restore that temple to the ancient truths. The measure of that restoration lies in the extent to which we apply social values more noble than mere monetary profit.

Happiness lies not in the mere possession of money; it lies in the joy of achievement, in the thrill of creative effort. The joy, the moral stimulation of work no longer must be forgotten in the mad chase of evanescent profits. These dark days, my friends, will be worth all they cost us if they teach us that our true destiny is not to be ministered unto but to minister to ourselves, to our fellow men.

Recognition of that falsity of material wealth as the standard of success goes hand in hand with the abandonment of the false belief that public office and high political position are to be valued only by the standards of pride of place and personal profit; and there must be an end to a conduct in banking and in business which too often has given to a sacred trust the likeness of callous and selfish wrongdoing. Small wonder that confidence languishes, for it thrives only on honesty, on honor, on the sacredness of obligations, on faithful protection, and on unselfish performance; without them it cannot live.

Restoration calls, however, not for changes in ethics alone. This nation is asking for action, and action now.

Our greatest primary task is to put people to work. This is no unsolvable problem if we face it wisely and courageously. It can be accomplished in part by direct recruiting by the Government itself, treating the task as we would treat the emergency of a war, but at the same time, through this employment, accomplishing great – greatly needed projects to stimulate and reorganize the use of our great natural resources […]

Yes, the task can be helped by definite efforts to raise the values of agricultural products, and with this the power to purchase the output of our cities. It can be helped by preventing realistically the tragedy of the growing loss through foreclosure of our small homes and our farms. It can be helped by insistence that the Federal, the State, and the local governments act forthwith on the demand that their cost be drastically reduced. It can be helped by the unifying of relief activities which today are often scattered, uneconomical, unequal. It can be helped by national planning for and supervision of all forms of transportation and of communications and other utilities that have a definitely public character. There are many ways in which it can be helped, but it can never be helped by merely talking about it […]

And finally, in our progress towards a resumption of work, we require two safeguards against a return of the evils of the old order. There must be a strict supervision of all banking and credits and investments. There must be an end to speculation with other people's money. And there must be provision for an adequate but sound currency […]

Through this program of action we address ourselves to putting our own national house in order and making income balance outgo. Our international trade relations, though vastly important, are in point of time, and necessity, secondary to the establishment of a sound national economy. I favor, as a practical policy, the putting of first things first. I shall spare no effort to restore world trade by international economic readjustment; but the emergency at home cannot wait on that accomplishment.

The basic thought that guides these specific means of national recovery is not nationally – narrowly nationalistic. It is the insistence, as a first consideration, upon the interdependence of the various elements in and parts of the United States of America – a recognition of the old and permanently important manifestation of the American spirit of the pioneer. It is the way to recovery. It is the immediate way. It is the strongest assurance that recovery will endure.

In the field of world policy, I would dedicate this Nation to the policy of the good neighbor: the neighbor who resolutely respects himself and, because he does so, respects the rights of others; the neighbour who respects his obligations and respects the sanctity of his agreements in and with a world of neighbors [...]

We are, I know, ready and willing to submit our lives and our property to such discipline, because it makes possible a leadership which aims at the larger good. This, I propose to offer, pledging that the larger purposes will bind upon us, bind upon us all as a sacred obligation with a unity of duty hitherto evoked only in times of armed strife.

With this pledge taken, I assume unhesitatingly the leadership of this great army of our people dedicated to a disciplined attack upon our common problems.

Action in this image, action to this end is feasible under the form of government which we have inherited from our ancestors. Our Constitution is so simple, so practical that it is possible always to meet extraordinary needs by changes in emphasis and arrangement without loss of essential form. That is why our constitutional system has proved itself the most superbly enduring political mechanism the modern world has ever seen.

It has met every stress of vast expansion of territory, of foreign wars, of bitter internal strife, of world relations. And it is to be hoped that the normal balance of executive and legislative authority may be wholly equal, wholly adequate to meet the unprecedented task before us. But it may be that an unprecedented demand and need for undelayed action may call for temporary departure from that normal balance of public procedure.

I am prepared under my constitutional duty to recommend the measures that a stricken nation in the midst of a stricken world may require. These measures, or such other measures as the Congress may build out of its experience and wisdom, I shall seek, within my constitutional authority, to bring to speedy adoption [...]

For the trust reposed in me, I will return the courage and the devotion that befit the time. I can do no less [...]

In this dedication – In this dedication of a Nation, we humbly ask the blessing of God.

May He protect each and every one of us.

May He guide me in the days to come.

Harry S. Truman

1884–1972

33rd President: April 12, 1945–January 20, 1953

On April 16, 1945 – the day after President Franklin D. Roosevelt's funeral – his successor President Harry S. Truman addressed a joint session of Congress and the speech was broadcast to the nation. In it, he pledged to carry on President Roosevelt's work and to keep true to the ideals of the American people. Less than a month later, Germany had surrendered, and the war would be over in four months, once the Japanese Emperor capitulated. America had poured so many resources into the war that it would take the economy years to recover, and Truman is remembered as much for the Marshall Plan as the foundation of both NATO and the United Nations (UN).

It is with a heavy heart that I stand before you, my friends and colleagues, in the Congress of the United States [...]

In His infinite wisdom, Almighty God has seen fit to take from us a great man who loved, and was beloved by, all humanity. No man could possibly fill the tremendous void left by the passing of that noble soul [...]

Tragic fate has thrust upon us grave responsibilities. We must carry on. Our departed leader never looked backward. He looked forward and moved forward. That is what he would want us to do. That is what America will do.

So much blood has already been shed for the ideals which we cherish, and for which Franklin Delano Roosevelt lived and died, that we dare not permit even a momentary pause in the hard fight for victory [...]

So that there can be no possible misunderstanding, both Germany and Japan can be certain, beyond any shadow of a doubt, that America will continue the fight for freedom until no vestige of resistance remains! We are deeply conscious of the fact that much hard fighting is still ahead of us.

Having to pay such a heavy price to make complete victory certain, America will never become a party to any plan for partial victory!

To settle for merely another temporary respite would surely jeopardize the future security of all the world.

Our demand has been, and it remains – Unconditional Surrender! We will not traffic with the breakers of the peace on the terms of the peace.

The responsibility for making of the peace – and it is a very grave responsibility – must rest with the defenders of the peace. We are not unconscious of the dictates of humanity. We do not wish to see unnecessary or unjustified suffering. But the laws of God and of man have been violated and the guilty must not go unpunished. Nothing shall shake our determination to punish the war criminals even though we must pursue them to the ends of the earth.

Lasting peace can never be secured if we permit our dangerous opponents to plot future wars with impunity at any mountain retreat – however distant [...]

In the difficult days ahead, unquestionably we shall face problems of staggering proportions. However, with the faith of our fathers in our hearts, we do not fear the future.

On the battlefields, we have frequently faced overwhelming odds – and won! At home, Americans will not be less resolute!

We shall never cease our struggle to preserve and maintain our American way of life.

At this moment, America, along with her brave Allies, is paying again a heavy price for the defense of our freedom. With characteristic energy, we are assisting in the liberation of entire nations. Gradually, the shackles of slavery are being broken by the forces of freedom [...]

I want the entire world to know that this direction must and will remain unchanged and unhampered!

Our forefathers came to our rugged shores in search of religious tolerance, political freedom and economic opportunity. For those fundamental rights, they risked their lives. We well know today that such rights can be preserved only by constant vigilance, the eternal price of liberty!

In the memory of those who have made the supreme sacrifice – in the memory of our fallen President – we shall not fail!

It is not enough to yearn for peace. We must work, and if necessary, fight for it [...]

Fortunately, people have retained hope for a durable peace. Thoughtful people have always had faith that ultimately justice must triumph. Past experience surely indicates that, without justice, an enduring peace becomes impossible [...]

During the dark hours of this horrible war, entire nations were kept going by something intangible – hope! When warned that abject submission offered the only salvation against overwhelming power, hope showed the way to victory.

Hope has become the secret weapon of the forces of liberation!

But hope alone was not and is not sufficient to avert war. We must not only have hope but we must have faith enough to work with other peace-loving nations to maintain the peace. Hope was not enough to beat back the aggressors as long as the peace-loving nations were unwilling to come to each other's defense. The aggressors were beaten back only when the peace-loving nations united to defend themselves.

If wars in the future are to be prevented the nations must be united in their determination to keep the peace under law [...]

To build a foundation of enduring peace we must not only work in harmony with our friends abroad, but we must have the united support of our own people [...]

I appeal to every American, regardless of party, race, creed, or color, to support our efforts to build a strong and lasting United Nations Organization [...] America must assist suffering humanity back along the path of peaceful progress. This will require time and tolerance. We shall need also an abiding faith in the people, the kind of faith and courage which Franklin Delano Roosevelt always had!

Today, America has become one of the most powerful forces for good on earth. We must keep it so. We have achieved a world leadership which does not depend solely upon our military and naval might.

We have learned to fight with other nations in common defense of our freedom.

We must now learn to live with other nations for our mutual good. We must learn to trade more with other nations so that there may be – for our mutual advantage – better standards of living throughout the world.

May we Americans all live up to our glorious heritage.

In that way, America may well lead the world to peace and prosperity.

At this moment, I have in my heart a prayer. As I have assumed my heavy duties, I humbly pray Almighty God, in the words of King Solomon:

"Give therefore thy servant an understanding heart to judge thy people, that I may discern between good and bad; for who is able to judge this thy so great a people?"

I ask only to be a good and faithful servant of my Lord and my people.

John F. Kennedy

1917–1963
35th President: January 20, 1961–November 22, 1963

In John F. Kennedy's inaugural speech, on January 20, 1961, the young president used the founding of the U.S.A. as an inspirational notion with which to promote his vision and plans for the future. Unlike many of his predecessors, who spoke chiefly of domestic concerns and seemed to want to be uninvolved with the rest of the world, JFK talked of his aspirations for both America and other nations. The most remembered line of the speech is: "And so, my fellow Americans, ask not what your country can do for you; ask what you can do for your country." But it is followed by the less well-known, but just as pivotal: "My fellow citizens of the world, ask not what America will do for you, but what together we can do for the freedom of man."

Vice President Johnson, Mr. Speaker, Mr. Chief Justice, President Eisenhower, Vice President Nixon, President Truman, Reverend Clergy, fellow citizens:

We observe today not a victory of party but a celebration of freedom –

symbolizing an end as well as a beginning – signifying renewal as well as change. For I have sworn before you and Almighty God the same solemn oath our forebears prescribed nearly a century and three-quarters ago.

The world is very different now. For man holds in his mortal hands the power to abolish all forms of human poverty and all forms of human life. And yet the same revolutionary beliefs for which our forebears fought are still at issue around the globe – the belief that the rights of man come not from the generosity of the state but from the hand of God.

We dare not forget today that we are the heirs of that first revolution. Let the word go forth from this time and place, to friend and foe alike, that the torch has been passed to a new generation of Americans – born in this century, tempered by war, disciplined by a hard and bitter peace, proud of our ancient heritage – and unwilling to witness or permit the slow undoing of those human rights to which this nation has always been committed, and to which we are committed today at home and around the world.

Let every nation know, whether it wishes us well or ill, that we shall pay any price, bear any burden, meet any hardship, support any friend, oppose any foe to assure the survival and the success of liberty.

This much we pledge – and more. To those old allies whose cultural and spiritual origins we share, we pledge the loyalty of faithful friends. United there is little we cannot do in a host of cooperative ventures. Divided there is little we can do – for we dare not meet a powerful challenge at odds and split asunder.

To those new states whom we welcome to the ranks of the free, we pledge our word that one form of colonial control shall not have passed away merely to be replaced by a far more iron tyranny. We shall not always expect to find them supporting our view. But we shall always hope to find them strongly supporting their own freedom – and to remember that, in the past, those who foolishly sought power by riding the back of the tiger ended up inside.

To those people in the huts and villages of half the globe struggling to break the bonds of mass misery, we pledge our best efforts to help them help themselves, for whatever period is required – not because the Communists may be doing it, not because we seek their votes, but because it is right. If a free society cannot help the many who are poor, it cannot save the few who are rich.

To our sister republics south of our border, we offer a special pledge – to convert our good words into good deeds – in a new alliance for progress – to assist free men and free governments in casting off the chains of poverty. But this peaceful revolution of hope cannot become the prey of hostile powers. Let all our neighbors know that we shall join with them to oppose aggression or subversion anywhere in the Americas. And let every other power know that this hemisphere intends to remain the master of its own house.

To that world assembly of sovereign states, the United Nations, our last best hope in an age where the instruments of war have far outpaced the instruments of peace, we renew our pledge of support – to prevent it from becoming merely a forum for invective – to strengthen its shield of the new and the weak – and to enlarge the area in which its writ may run.

Finally, to those nations who would make themselves our adversary, we offer not a pledge but a request: that both sides begin anew the quest for peace, before the dark powers of destruction unleashed by science engulf all humanity in planned or accidental self-destruction.

We dare not tempt them with weakness. For only when our arms are sufficient beyond doubt can we be certain beyond doubt that they will never be employed.

But neither can two great and powerful groups of nations take comfort from our present course – both sides overburdened by the cost of modern weapons, both rightly alarmed by the steady spread of the deadly atom, yet both racing to alter that uncertain balance of terror that stays the hand of mankind's final war.

So let us begin anew – remembering on both sides that civility is not a sign of weakness, and sincerity is always subject to proof. Let us never negotiate out of fear. But let us never fear to negotiate.

Let both sides explore what problems unite us instead of belabouring those problems which divide us.

Let both sides, for the first time, formulate serious and precise proposals for the inspection and control of arms – and bring the absolute power to destroy other nations under the absolute control of all nations.

Let both sides seek to invoke the wonders of science instead of its terrors. Together let us explore the stars, conquer the deserts, eradicate disease, tap the ocean depths and encourage the arts and commerce.

Let both sides unite to heed in all corners of the earth the command of Isaiah – to "undo the heavy burdens […] (and) let the oppressed go free."

And if a beachhead of cooperation may push back the jungle of suspicion, let both sides join in creating a new endeavour, not a new balance of power, but a new world of law, where the strong are just and the weak secure and the peace preserved.

All this will not be finished in the first one hundred days. Nor will it be finished in the first one thousand days, nor in the life of this Administration, nor even perhaps in our lifetime on this planet. But let us begin.

In your hands, my fellow citizens, more than mine, will rest the final success or failure of our course. Since this country was founded, each generation of Americans has been summoned to give testimony to its national loyalty. The graves of young Americans who answered the call to service surround the globe.

Now the trumpet summons us again – not as a call to bear arms, though arms we need – not as a call to battle, though embattled we are – but a call to bear the burden of a long twilight struggle, year in and year out, "rejoicing in hope, patient in tribulation" – a struggle against the common enemies of man: tyranny, poverty, disease and war itself.

Can we forge against these enemies a grand and global alliance, north and south, east and west, that can assure a more fruitful life for all mankind? Will you join in that historic effort?

In the long history of the world, only a few generations have been granted the role of defending freedom in its hour of maximum danger. I do not shrink from this responsibility – I welcome it. I do not believe that any of us would exchange places with any other people or any other generation. The energy, the faith, the devotion which we bring to this endeavour will light our country and all who serve it – and the glow from that fire can truly light the world.

And so, my fellow Americans: ask not what your country can do for you – ask what you can do for your country.

My fellow citizens of the world: ask not what America will do for you, but what together we can do for the freedom of man.

Finally, whether you are citizens of America or citizens of the world, ask of us here the same high standards of strength and sacrifice which we ask of you. With a good conscience our only sure reward, with history the final judge of our deeds, let us go forth to lead the land we love, asking His blessing and His help, but knowing that here on earth God's work must truly be our own.

Gerald Ford

—————•—————

1913–2006
38th President: August 9, 1974–January 20, 1977

Gerald Ford, the successor to Richard Nixon, is the only person in U.S. history to become first vice president and then president without ever being actually elected to either position. At 895 days, his presidency is so far the shortest of any incumbent other than those who died in office. In these remarks, Ford took pains to assure the American people that he would do his best to draw a line under the scandals of the Nixon era and move the country on to a more positive phase. However, his pardoning of Nixon soon tarnished his reputation for honesty and after a presidency embattled by a faltering economy, he lost the 1976 election to Jimmy Carter.

Mr. Chief Justice, my dear friends, my fellow Americans:

The oath that I have taken is the same oath that was taken by George Washington and by every President under the Constitution. But I assume the Presidency under extraordinary circumstances never before experienced by Americans. This is an hour of history that troubles our minds and hurts our hearts.

Therefore, I feel it is my first duty to make an unprecedented compact with my countrymen. Not an inaugural address, not a fireside chat, not a campaign speech – just a little straight talk among friends. And I intend it to be the first of many.

I am acutely aware that you have not elected me as your President by your ballots, and so I ask you to confirm me as your President with your prayers. And I hope that such prayers will also be the first of many.

If you have not chosen me by secret ballot, neither have I gained office by any secret promises. I have not campaigned either for the Presidency or the Vice Presidency. I have not subscribed to any partisan platform. I am indebted to no man, and only to one woman – my dear wife – as I begin this very difficult job.

I have not sought this enormous responsibility, but I will not shirk it. Those who nominated and confirmed me as Vice President were my friends and are my friends. They were of both parties, elected by all the people and acting under the

Constitution in their name. It is only fitting then that I should pledge to them and to you that I will be the President of all the people.

Thomas Jefferson said the people are the only sure reliance for the preservation of our liberty. And down the years, Abraham Lincoln renewed this American article of faith asking, "Is there any better way or equal hope in the world?"

I intend, on Monday next, to request of the Speaker of the House of Representatives and the President pro tempore of the Senate the privilege of appearing before the Congress to share with my former colleagues and with you, the American people, my views on the priority business of the Nation and to solicit your views and their views. And may I say to the Speaker and the others, if I could meet with you right after these remarks, I would appreciate it.

Even though this is late in an election year, there is no way we can go forward except together and no way anybody can win except by serving the people's urgent needs. We cannot stand still or slip backwards. We must go forward now together.

To the peoples and the governments of all friendly nations, and I hope that could encompass the whole world, I pledge an uninterrupted and sincere search for peace. America will remain strong and united, but its strength will remain dedicated to the safety and sanity of the entire family of man, as well as to our own precious freedom.

I believe that truth is the glue that holds government together, not only our Government but civilization itself. That bond, though strained, is unbroken at home and abroad.

In all my public and private acts as your President, I expect to follow my instincts of openness and candor with full confidence that honesty is always the best policy in the end.

My fellow Americans, our long national nightmare is over.

Our Constitution works; our great Republic is a government of laws and not of men. Here the people rule. But there is a higher Power, by whatever name we honor Him, who ordains not only righteousness but love, not only justice but mercy.

As we bind up the internal wounds of Watergate, more painful and more poisonous than those of foreign wars, let us restore the golden rule to our political process, and let brotherly love purge our hearts of suspicion and of hate.

In the beginning, I asked you to pray for me. Before closing, I ask again your prayers, for Richard Nixon and for his family. May our former President, who brought peace to millions, find it for himself. May God bless and comfort his wonderful wife and daughters, whose love and loyalty will forever be a shining legacy to all who bear the lonely burdens of the White House.

Ronald Reagan

1911–2004
40th President: January 20, 1981–January 20, 1989

As President Ronald Reagan was giving his inauguration speech, another important event for America was taking place – the end of the longest hostage crisis in recorded history, as 52 U.S. diplomats and citizens were flown out of Iran after 444 days of imprisonment following the takeover of the U.S. Embassy in Tehran by the Muslim Student Followers of the Imam's Line, a group supporting the Islamic Revolution.

Reagan broke the news during the inauguration lunch, speaking a short and heartfelt few lines that touch both on the joy of the event itself and on the importance of the "tag line" – essentially the sound bite – in contemporary politics.

With thanks to Almighty God, I have been given a tag line, the get-off line, that everyone wants for the end of a toast or a speech, or anything else. Some 30 minutes ago, the planes bearing our prisoners left Iranian air space, and they're now free of Iran.

George H. W. Bush

1924
41st President: January 20, 1989–January 20, 1993

George H. W. Bush ascended to the presidency at a time of hope for America. The Soviet Union was in its last days, and Marxism as a serious alternative to capitalism was on its way out. With sound bites like the idea of making "kinder the face of the Nation." he effectively presented U.S. national interest and moral behavior as natural partners. President Bush focused attention on voluntary service as a way of addressing social problems, using the image of a "thousand points of light" to celebrate the community groups doing good across America. Nevertheless, within two years of his inaugurations the U.S. was embroiled in the Gulf War.

America today is a proud, free nation, decent and civil, a place we cannot help but love. We know in our hearts, not loudly and proudly but as a simple fact, that this country has meaning beyond what we see, and that our strength is a force for good. But have we changed as a nation even in our time? Are we enthralled with material things, less appreciative of the nobility of work and sacrifice?

My friends, we are not the sum of our possessions. They are not the measure of our lives. In our hearts we know what matters. We cannot hope only to leave our children a bigger car, a bigger bank account. We must hope to give them a sense of what it means to be a loyal friend; a loving parent; a citizen who leaves his home, his neighborhood, and town better than he found it. And what do we want the men and women who work with us to say when we're no longer there? That we were more driven to succeed than anyone around us? Or that we stopped to ask if a sick child had gotten better and stayed a moment there to trade a word of friendship?

No President, no government can teach us to remember what is best in what we are. But if the man you have chosen to lead this government can help make a difference; if he can celebrate the quieter, deeper successes that are made not of gold and silk but of better hearts and finer souls; if he can do these things, then he must.

America is never wholly herself unless she is engaged in high moral principle. We as a people have such a purpose today. It is to make kinder the face of the Nation and gentler the face of the world. My friends, we have work to do […]

[…] Some see leadership as high drama and the sound of trumpets calling, and sometimes it is that. But I see history as a book with many pages, and each day we fill a page with acts of hopefulness and meaning. The new breeze blows, a page turns, the story unfolds. And so, today a chapter begins, a small and stately story of unity, diversity, and generosity – shared, and written, together.

Bill Clinton

1946
42nd President: January 20, 1993–January 20, 2001

In the immediate aftermath of the fall of the Soviet Union in late 1991, there were great hopes of a New World Order in which Russia would be a friendly country and the U.S. could focus on domestic problems without fear of world war.

As the first Democratic president for 12 years, Bill Clinton stressed a need for social and economic support structures in his inaugural speech, and wedded this to the national spirit by presenting the latter as something that could be harnessed to address the former. In the early days of his presidency, he increased taxes on the rich and succeeded in lowering the deficit from $290 billion in 1992 to $203 billion by 1994.

Profound and powerful forces are shaking and remaking our world, and the urgent question of our time is whether we can make change our friend and not our enemy.

This new world has enriched the lives of millions of Americans who are able to compete and win in it. But when people are working harder for less; when others cannot work at all; when the cost of health care devastates families and threatens to bankrupt enterprises, great and small; when fear of crime robs law-abiding citizens of their freedom; and when millions of poor children cannot even imagine the lives we are calling them to lead – we have not made change our friend.

We know we have to face hard truths and take strong steps. But we have not done so. Instead, we have drifted, and that drifting has eroded our resources, fractured our economy, and shaken our confidence.

Though our challenges are fearsome, so are our strengths. And Americans have ever been a restless, questing, hopeful people. We must bring to our task today the vision and the will of those who came before us.

From our Revolution, Civil War, to the Great Depression, to the Civil Rights Movement, our people have mustered the determination to construct from crises the pillars of our history.

Thomas Jefferson believed that to preserve the very foundations of our nation, we would need dramatic change from time to time. Well, my fellow citizens, this is our time. Let us embrace it.

Our democracy must not only be the envy of the world but the engine of our own renewal. There is nothing wrong with America that cannot be fixed by what is right with America.

And so today, we pledge an end to the era of deadlock and drift – a new season of American renewal has begun.

To renew America, we must be bold.

We must do what no generation has had to do before. We must invest more in our own people, in their jobs, in their future, and at the same time cut our massive debt.

We must do so in a world in which we must compete for every opportunity.

It will not be easy; it will require sacrifice. But it can be done, and done fairly, not choosing the sacrifice for it's own sake, but for our own sake, but for our own sake.

We must provide for our nation the way a family provides for it's children.

Our founders saw themselves in the light of posterity. We can do no less. Anyone who has ever watched a child's eyes wander into sleep knows what posterity is.

Posterity is the world to come – the world for whom we hold our ideals, from whom we have borrowed our planet, and to whom we bear sacred responsibility.

We must do what America does best; offer more opportunity to all and demand more responsibility of all.

It is time to break the bad habit of expecting something for nothing, from our government or from each other. Let us all take more responsibility, not only for ourselves and for our families but for our communities and for our country.

To renew America, we must revitalize our democracy.

This beautiful capital, like every capital since the dawn of civilization, is often a place of intrigue and calculation. Powerful people maneuver for position and worry endlessly about who is in and who is out, who is up and who is down, forgetting those whose toil and sweat sends us here and pays our way.

Americans deserve better, and in this city today, there are people who want to do better. Let us resolve to reform our politics, so that power and privilege no longer shout down the voice of the people. Let us put aside personal advantage so that we can feel the pain and see the promise of America.

Barack Obama

1961
44th President: January 20, 2009–January 20, 2017

In comparison to the upbeat nature of his acceptance speech on November 4, 2008, President Barack Obama's Inaugural Address was a sober call to restore responsibility – both political and personal – and a pledge to bring about change while respecting the traditions and values of the American people. On a freezing Washington day, standing behind a bullet-proof shield and looking out over the estimated 1,800,000 people on the National Mall stretching towards the Washington Monument, the new president spoke the following words.

That we are in the midst of crisis is now well understood. Our nation is at war, against a far-reaching network of violence and hatred. Our economy is badly weakened, a consequence of greed and irresponsibility on the part of some, but also our collective failure to make hard choices and prepare the nation for a new age. Homes have been lost; jobs shed; businesses shuttered. Our health care is too costly; our schools fail too many; and each day brings further evidence that the ways we use energy strengthen our adversaries and threaten our planet. These are the indicators of crisis, subject to data and statistics. Less measurable but no less profound is a sapping of confidence across our land – a nagging fear that America's decline is inevitable, and that the next generation must lower its sights.

Today, I say to you that the challenges we face are real. They are serious and they are many. They will not be met easily or in a short span of time. But know this, America – they will be met. On this day, we gather because we have chosen hope over fear, unity of purpose over conflict and discord.

On this day, we come to proclaim an end to the petty grievances and false promises, the recriminations and worn out dogmas, that for far too long have strangled our politics. We remain a young nation, but in the words of Scripture, the time has come to set aside childish things. The time has come to reaffirm our enduring spirit; to choose our better history; to carry forward that precious gift, that noble idea, passed on from generation to generation: the God-given promise that all are equal, all are free, and all deserve a chance to pursue their full measure of happiness.

In reaffirming the greatness of our nation, we understand that greatness is never a given. It must be earned. Our journey has never been one of short-cuts or settling for less. It has not been the path for the faint-hearted – for those who prefer leisure over work, or seek only the pleasures of riches and fame.

Rather, it has been the risk-takers, the doers, the makers of things – some celebrated but more often men and women obscure in their labor, who have carried us up the long, rugged path towards prosperity and freedom [...]

This is the journey we continue today. We remain the most prosperous, powerful nation on Earth. Our workers are no less productive than when this crisis began. Our minds are no less inventive, our goods and services no less needed than they were last week or last month or last year. Our capacity remains undiminished.

But our time of standing pat, of protecting narrow interests and putting off unpleasant decisions – that time has surely passed. Starting today, we must pick ourselves up, dust ourselves off, and begin again the work of remaking America.

For everywhere we look, there is work to be done. The state of the economy calls for action, bold and swift, and we will act – not only to create new jobs, but to lay a new foundation for growth. We will build the roads and bridges, the electric grids and digital lines that feed our commerce and bind us together. We will restore science to its rightful place, and wield technology's wonders to raise health care's quality and lower its cost. We will harness the sun and the winds and the soil to fuel our cars and run our factories. And we will transform our schools and colleges and universities to meet the demands of a new age. All this we can do. And all this we will do.

Now, there are some who question the scale of our ambitions – who suggest that our system cannot tolerate too many big plans. Their memories are short. For they have forgotten what this country has already done; what free men and women can achieve when imagination is joined to common purpose, and necessity to courage. What the cynics fail to understand is that the ground has shifted beneath them – that the stale political arguments that have consumed us for so long no longer apply.   The question we ask today is not whether our government is too big or too small, but whether it works – whether it helps families find jobs at a decent wage, care they can afford, a retirement that is dignified. Where the answer is yes, we intend to move forward. Where the answer is no, programs will end. And those of us who manage the public's dollars will be held to account – to spend wisely, reform bad habits, and do our business in the light of day – because only then can we restore the vital trust between a people and their government.

Nor is the question before us whether the market is a force for good or ill. Its power to generate wealth and expand freedom is unmatched, but this crisis has reminded us that without a watchful eye, the market can spin out of control – and that a nation cannot prosper long when it favors only the prosperous. The success of our economy has always depended not just on the size of our gross domestic product, but on the reach of our prosperity; on our ability to extend opportunity to every willing heart – not out of charity, but because it is the surest route to our common good. As for our common defense, we reject as false the choice between our safety and our ideals. Our Founding Fathers, faced with perils we can scarcely imagine, drafted a charter to assure the rule of law and the rights of man, a charter expanded by the blood of generations. Those ideals still light the world, and we will not give them up for expedience's sake. And so to all other peoples and governments who are watching today, from the grandest capitals to the small village where my father was born: know that America is a friend of each nation and every man, woman, and child who seeks a future of peace and dignity, and that we are ready to lead once more. Recall that earlier generations faced down fascism and communism not just with missiles and tanks, but with sturdy alliances and enduring convictions. They understood that our power alone cannot protect us, nor does it entitle us to do as we please. Instead, they knew that our power grows through its prudent use; our security emanates from the justness of our cause, the force of our example, the tempering qualities of humility and restraint.

We are the keepers of this legacy. Guided by these principles once more, we can meet those new threats that demand even greater effort – even greater cooperation and understanding between nations. We will begin to responsibly leave Iraq to its people, and forge a hard-earned peace in Afghanistan. With old friends and former foes, we will work tirelessly to lessen the nuclear threat, and roll back the spectre of a warming planet. We will not apologize for our way of life, nor will we waver in its defense, and for those who seek to advance their aims by inducing terror and slaughtering innocents, we say to you now that our spirit is stronger and cannot be broken; you cannot outlast us, and we will defeat you. For we know that our patchwork heritage is a strength, not a weakness. We are a nation of Christians and Muslims, Jews and Hindus – and non-believers. We are shaped by every language and culture, drawn from every end of this Earth; and because we have tasted the bitter swill of civil war and segregation, and emerged from that dark chapter stronger and more united, we cannot help but believe that the old hatreds shall someday pass; that the lines of tribe shall soon dissolve; that as the world grows smaller, our common humanity shall reveal itself; and that America must play its role in ushering in a new era of peace. To the Muslim world, we seek a new way forward, based on mutual interest and mutual respect. To those leaders around the globe who seek to sow conflict, or blame their society's ills on the West – know that your people will judge you on what you can build, not what you destroy. To those who cling to power through corruption and deceit and the silencing of dissent, know that you are on the wrong side of history; but that we will extend a hand if you are willing to unclench your fist. To the people of poor nations, we pledge to work alongside you to make your farms flourish and let clean waters flow; to nourish starved bodies and feed hungry minds. And to those nations like ours that enjoy relative plenty, we say we can no longer afford indifference to suffering outside our borders; nor can we consume the world's resources without regard to effect. For the world has changed, and we must change with it. As we consider the road that unfolds before us, we remember with humble gratitude those brave Americans who, at this very hour, patrol far-off deserts and distant mountains. They have something to tell us today, just as the fallen heroes who lie in Arlington whisper through the ages. We honor them not only because they are guardians of our liberty, but because they embody the spirit of service; a willingness to find meaning in something greater than themselves. And yet, at this moment – a moment that will define a generation – it is precisely this spirit that must inhabit us all. For as much as government can do and must do, it is ultimately the faith and determination of the American people upon which this nation relies. It is the kindness to take in a stranger when the levees break, the selflessness of workers who would rather cut their hours than see a friend lose their job which sees us through our darkest hours. It is the fire-fighter's courage to storm a stairway filled with smoke, but also a parent's willingness to nurture a child, that finally decides our fate. Our challenges may be new. The instruments with which we meet them may be new. But those values upon which our success depends – hard work and honesty, courage and fair play, tolerance and curiosity, loyalty and patriotism – these things are old. These things are true. They have been the quiet force of progress throughout our history. What is demanded then is a return to these truths. What is required of us now is a new era of responsibility – a recognition, on the part of every American, that we have duties to ourselves, our nation, and the world, duties that we do not grudgingly accept but rather seize gladly, firm in the knowledge that there is nothing so satisfying to the spirit, so defining of our character, than giving our all to a difficult task. This is the price and the promise of citizenship.

STATE OF THE UNION ADDRESSES

James Monroe

1758–1831
5th President: March 4, 1817–March 4, 1825

On December 2, 1823, President James Monroe gave his seventh State of the Union Address. Within it were proposals for how the U.S.A. should conduct foreign relations: namely, that friendly relations should be maintained as far as possible but the U.S.A. would not intervene in European wars and, as such, expected European nations to keep their noses out of Central and Southern America. Any attempt by a former colonial power to regain influence in the region would be regarded as a direct threat to the U.S. and would be treated as such. The basic tenets of the Monroe Doctrine have governed much of U.S.A. foreign policy ever since.

[…] In the discussions to which this interest has given rise and in the arrangements by which they may terminate the occasion has been judged proper for asserting, as a principle in which the rights and interests of the United States are involved, that the American continents, by the free and independent condition which they have assumed and maintain, are henceforth not to be considered as subjects for future colonization by any European powers […]

It was stated at the commencement of the last session that a great effort was then making in Spain and Portugal to improve the condition of the people of those countries, and that it appeared to be conducted with extraordinary moderation. It need scarcely be remarked that the results have been so far very different from what was then anticipated. Of events in that quarter of the globe, with which we have so much intercourse and from which we derive our origin, we have always been anxious and interested spectators. The citizens of the United States cherish sentiments the most friendly in favor of the liberty and happiness of their fellow-men on that side of the Atlantic. In the wars of the European powers in matters relating to themselves we have never taken any part, nor does it comport with our policy to do so. It is only when our rights are invaded or seriously menaced that we resent injuries or make preparation for our defense. With the movements in this hemisphere we are of necessity more immediately connected, and by causes which must be obvious to all enlightened and impartial observers

[...] We owe it, therefore, to candor and to the amicable relations existing between the United States and those powers to declare that we should consider any attempt on their part to extend their system to any portion of this hemisphere as dangerous to our peace and safety. With the existing colonies or dependencies of any European power we have not interfered and shall not interfere. But with the Governments who have declared their independence and maintain it, and whose independence we have, on great consideration and on just principles, acknowledged, we could not view any interposition for the purpose of oppressing them, or controlling in any other manner their destiny, by any European power in any other light than as the manifestation of an unfriendly disposition toward the United States [...]

Our policy in regard to Europe, which was adopted at an early stage of the wars which have so long agitated that quarter of the globe, nevertheless remains the same, which is, not to interfere in the internal concerns of any of its powers; to consider the government de facto as the legitimate government for us; to cultivate friendly relations with it, and to preserve those relations by a frank, firm, and manly policy, meeting in all instances the just claims of every power, submitting to injuries from none. But in regard to those continents circumstances are eminently and conspicuously different. It is impossible that the allied powers should extend their political system to any portion of either continent without endangering our peace and happiness; nor can anyone believe that our southern brethren, if left to themselves, would adopt it of their own accord. It is equally impossible, therefore, that we should behold such interposition in any form with indifference. If we look to the comparative strength and resources of Spain and those new Governments, and their distance from each other, it must be obvious that she can never subdue them. It is still the true policy of the United States to leave the parties to themselves, in hope that other powers will pursue the same course [...]

Andrew Jackson

1767–1845
7th President: March 4, 1829–March 4, 1837

In May 1830, President AndrewJackson had signed into force the Indian Removal Act, which had support from a broad base of white people, especially in southern states in need of extra land. It legislated for the exchange of Indian land for lands farther west. On December 6, the President reported back to Congress that two tribes – the Choctaw and the Chickasaw – had signed removal treaties. It had been clear to most when the Bill was being debated – although not to the chiefs who were pressured into signing removal treaties – that the removals would inevitably be forced, not voluntary. During the 1838 forced removal of the Cherokees, more than 4,000 of the 15,000-strong people died in transit camps or en route to what is now Oklahoma.

It gives me pleasure to announce to Congress that the benevolent policy of the Government, steadily pursued for nearly 30 years, in relation to the removal of the Indians beyond the white settlements is approaching a happy consummation. Two important tribes have accepted the provision made for their removal at the last session of Congress, and it is believed that their example will induce the remaining tribes also to seek the same obvious advantages [...]

The consequences of a speedy removal will be important to the United States, to individual States, and to the Indians themselves. The pecuniary advantages which it promises to the government are the least of its recommendations. It puts an end to all possible danger of collision between the authorities of the general and State governments, on account of the Indians. It will place a dense and civilized population in large tracts of country now occupied by a few savage hunters. By opening the whole territory between Tennessee on the north, and Louisiana on the south, to the settlements of the whites, it will incalculably strengthen the southwestern frontier, and render the adjacent States strong enough to repel future invasion without remote aid. It will relieve the whole State of Mississippi, and the western part of Alabama, of Indian occupancy and enable those States to advance rapidly in population, wealth, and power. It will separate the Indians from immediate contact with settlements of whites; free them from the power of the States; enable to pursue happiness in their own way and under their own rude institutions; will retard the progress of decay, which is lessening their numbers; and perhaps cause them gradually, under the protection of the government, and through the influence of good counsels, to cast off their savage habits and become an interesting, civilized, and Christian community. These consequences, some of them so certain, and the rest so probably, make the complete execution of the plan sanctioned by Congress at their last session an object of much solicitude.

John Tyler

1790–1862
10th President: April 4, 1841–March 4, 1845

Long before McCarthyism, there was fear of infiltration of American politics by malign outside influences, and admonishments against foreign influence were a familiar theme in presidential addresses of the 1830s and 1840s. In those days, however, the subtext was usually a warning to Britain to keep its nose out of U.S. business. As president, John Tyler was a supporter both of U.S. autonomy and the rights of individual states, avoiding infringing on them in his policies. He advocated free trade and expansionism toward the Pacific, while increasing the strength of the navy. Before the Civil War, America's unity had yet to be tested, and expansionist optimism and national identity was still strong.

One of the strongest objections which has been urged against confederacies by writers on government is the liability of the members to be tampered with by foreign governments or the people of foreign states, either in their local affairs or in such as affected the peace of others or endangered the safety of the whole confederacy. We can not hope to be entirely exempt from such attempts on our peace and safety. The United States are becoming too important in population and resources not to attract the observation of other nations. It therefore may in the progress of time occur that opinions entirely abstract in the States which they may prevail and in no degree affecting their domestic institutions may be artfully but secretly encouraged with a view to undermine the Union. Such opinions may become the foundation of political parties, until at last the conflict of opinion, producing an alienation of friendly feeling among the people of the different States, may involve in general destruction the happy institutions under which we live. It should ever be borne in mind that what is true in regard to individuals is equally so in regard to states. An interference of one in the affairs of another is the fruitful cause of family dissensions and neighborhood disputes, and the same cause affects the peace, happiness, and prosperity of states. It may be most devoutly hoped that the good sense of the American people will ever be ready to repel all such attempts should they ever be made.

Millard Fillmore

1800–1874
13th President: July 9, 1850–March 4, 1853

Millard Fillmore presided over a period of enterprise and further territorial expansion, with California entering the Union as the thirty-first state, in 1850. His 1852 State of the Union address touched on the questions raised and challenges posed by the rate of change, particularly in technology. In the final days of Fillmore's presidency, Congress was to authorize the railroad survey that was to lead to construction, in the 1860s, of a railroad running from Omaha, Nebraska, to San Francisco in the 1860s.

We live in an age of progress, and ours is emphatically a country of progress. Within the last half century the number of States in this Union has nearly doubled, the population has almost quadrupled, and our boundaries have been extended from the Mississippi to the Pacific. Our territory is checkered over with railroads and furrowed with canals. The inventive talent of our country is excited to the highest pitch, and the numerous applications for patents for valuable improvements distinguish this age and this people from all others. The genius of one American has enabled our commerce to move against wind and tide and that of another has annihilated distance in the transmission of intelligence. The whole country is full of enterprise. Our common schools are diffusing intelligence among the people and our industry is fast accumulating the comforts and luxuries of life. This is in part owing to our peculiar position, to our fertile soil and comparatively sparse population; but much of it is also owing to the popular institutions under which we live, to the freedom which every man feels to engage in any useful pursuit according to his taste or inclination, and to the entire confidence that his person and property will be protected by the laws. But whatever may be the cause of this unparalleled growth in population, intelligence, and wealth, one tiring is clear--that the Government must keep pace with the progress of the people. It must participate in their spirit of enterprise, and while it exacts obedience to the laws and restrains all unauthorized invasions of the rights of neighboring states, it should foster and protect home industry and lend its powerful strength to the improvement of such means of intercommunication as are necessary to promote our internal commerce and strengthen the ties which bind us together as a people.

Franklin Pierce

1804–1869
14th President: March 4, 1853–March 4, 1857

The absolutely central role of the American Constitution to the nation's identity was summed up by President Franklin Pierce in his third State of the Union address. Pierce's presidency came at a time of increasing tension between North and South, that was in 1861 to explode into civil war, and politicians on both sides were looking to the Constitution as an "unshaken rock."

The storm of frenzy and faction must inevitably dash itself in vain against the unshaken rock of the Constitution. I shall never doubt it

Ulysses S. Grant

1822–1885
18th President: March 4, 1869–March 4, 1877

Ulysses S. Grant's campaign slogan for the 1868 election, "Let us have peace," referred to both the reconstruction of the South, and relations with the Indian tribes in the west. "Peace" was one way of putting it; an only slightly blunter rephrasing of his discussion of the subject in his 1869 State of the Union address would be "killing them all would go too far so let's pen them up." Yet this was a kinder approach than the previous wars of extermination.

Indians were not forced to live on reservations: they could leave at any time and join the wider community, and become U.S. citizens. But any Indians doing so would be absorbed into white America – which was the goal of government policy.

The building of railroads, and the access thereby given to all the agricultural and mineral regions of the country, is rapidly bringing civilized settlements into contact with all the tribes of Indians. No matter what ought to be the relations between such settlements and the aborigines, the fact is they do not harmonize well, and one or the other has to give way in the end. A system which looks to the extinction of a race is too horrible for a nation to adopt without entailing upon itself the wrath of all Christendom and engendering in the citizen a disregard for human life and the rights of others, dangerous to society. I see no substitute for such a system, except in placing all the Indians on large reservations, as rapidly as it can be done, and giving them absolute protection there. As soon as they are fitted for it they should be induced to take their lands in severalty and to set up Territorial governments for their own protection.

Rutherford B. Hayes

1822–1893
19th President: March 4, 1877–March 4, 1881

Twentieth-century advances in medicine have freed us from the kind of catastrophe to which earlier communities were desperately vulnerable. This excerpt from Rutherford B. Hayes's second State of the Union speech is a glimpse of national disaster of a very particular kind: epidemic. In March 1879, in an effort to control the spread of disease, "An Act to Prevent the Introduction of Infectious or Contagious Disease into the United States and to Establish a National Board of Health" was passed, but the death of the Surgeon General Dr. John Woodworth soon afterwards left the organisation vulnerable to political jockeying and, in 1893, Congress failed to reauthorise it, in favour of increasing the powers of the Marine Hospital Service (MHS).

The enjoyment of health by our people generally has, however, been interrupted during the past season by the prevalence of a fatal pestilence (the yellow fever) in some portions of the Southern States, creating an emergency which called for prompt and extraordinary measures of relief. The disease appeared as an epidemic at New Orleans and at other places on the Lower Mississippi soon after midsummer. It was rapidly spread by fugitives from the infected cities and towns, and did not disappear until early in November. The States of Louisiana, Mississippi, and Tennessee have suffered severely. About 100,000 cases are believed to have occurred, of which about 20,000, according to intelligent estimates, proved fatal. It is impossible to estimate with any approach to accuracy the loss to the country occasioned by this epidemic It is to be reckoned by the hundred millions of dollars.

The suffering and destitution that resulted excited the deepest sympathy in all parts of the Union. Physicians and nurses hastened from every quarter to the assistance of the afflicted communities. Voluntary contributions of money and supplies, in every needed form, were speedily and generously furnished. The Government was able to respond in some measure to the call for help, by providing tents, medicines, and food for the sick and destitute, the requisite directions for the purpose being given in the confident expectation that this action of the Executive would receive the sanction of Congress. About 1,800 tents, and rations of the value of about $25,000, were sent to cities and towns which applied for them, full details of which will be furnished to Congress by the proper Department.

The fearful spread of this pestilence has awakened a very general public sentiment in favor of national sanitary administration, which shall not only control quarantine, but have the sanitary supervision of internal commerce in times of epidemics, and hold an advisory relation to the State and municipal health authorities, with power to deal with whatever endangers the public health, and which the municipal and State authorities are unable to regulate.

Chester Arthur

1829–1886
21st President: September 19, 1881–March 4, 1885

Chester Arthur was a reluctant president. As vice president, he inherited the job when President James A. Garfield died, and was as interested in hunting and fishing as in running the country. In 1883, he took a trip to Yellowstone National Park that was the focus of much public attention – Arthur suffered from Bright's disease, which affects the kidneys, so should he undertake such an arduous trip? He did so, and the influence of this trip and his love of nature could be seen in his 1883 State of the Union speech, which included pioneering measures to protect America's environment.

In my last annual message, I called attention to the necessity of protecting by suitable legislation the forests situated upon the public domain. In many portions of the West the pursuit of general agriculture is only made practicable by resort to irrigation, while successful irrigation would itself be impossible without the aid afforded by forests in contributing to the regularity and constancy of the supply of water.

During the past year severe suffering and great loss of property have been occasioned by profuse floods followed by periods of unusually low water in many of the great rivers of the country.

These irregularities were in great measure caused by the removal from about the sources of the streams in question of the timber by which the water supply had been nourished and protected.

The Preservation of such portions of the forests on the national domain as essentially contribute to the equable flow of important water courses is of the highest consequence.

Important tributaries of the Missouri, the Columbia, and the Saskatchewan rise in the mountain region of Montana, near the northern boundary of the United States, between the Blackfeet and Flathead Indian reservations. This region is unsuitable for settlement, but upon the rivers which flow from it depends the future agricultural development of a vast tract of country. The attention of Congress is called to the necessity of withdrawing from public sale this part of the public domain and establishing there a forest preserve.

Benjamin Harrison

1833–1901

23rd President: March 4, 1889–March 4, 1893

Like many presidencies of this period, Benjamin Harrison's was in part defined by the issue of African-American civil rights, of which he was a supporter. He reminded Congress, in December 1889, that "The colored people did not intrude themselves upon us; they were brought here in chains and held in communities where they are now chiefly bound by a cruel slave code." In his 1890 State of the Union speech, he put his finger on the psychological and social value of elections and the right to vote.

If any intelligent and loyal company of American citizens were required to catalogue the essential human conditions of national life, I do not doubt that with absolute unanimity they would begin with "free and honest elections."

William McKinley

1843–1901

25th President: March 4, 1897–September 14, 1901

The Library of Congress is the largest library in the world, with well over 160 million individual items in its catalogue today. It was established in 1800 by President John Adams, but not until the 1890s was a permanent home constructed. The project was begun a decade before William McKinley's presidency, but to him fell the honor of the formal opening.

Today, the library is housed on three different sites, all within New York City: the

Thomas Jefferson Building (the original Library of Congress Building, renamed in 1980), the John Adams Building and the James Madison Memorial Building.

The Library building provided for by the act of Congress approved April 15, 1886, has been completed and opened to the public. It should be a matter of congratulation that through the foresight and munificence of Congress the nation possesses this noble treasure-house of knowledge. It is earnestly to be hoped that having done so much toward the cause of education, Congress will continue to develop the Library in every phase of research to the end that it may be not only one of the most magnificent but among the richest and most useful libraries in the world.

Calvin Coolidge

1872–1933
30th President: August 2, 1923–March 4, 1929

In his first State of the Union Address on December 6, 1923, President Calvin Coolidge covered a variety of themes, including increased enforcement of Prohibition, infrastructure projects that would increase employment, wealth and trade, flexible trade tariffs, the removal of war taxes, cancellation of some foreign debts, continued lack of recognition of Russia, reform in the judicial and prison systems, marine environmental protection and fisheries regulation laws, strengthening of the army and navy, and entitlement for free health care for veterans. However, the speech's most far-reaching areas were those about foreign affairs, in which he definitively ruled out joining the League of Nations and said that America would only join a World Court of Justice on that condition.

Since the close of the last Congress the Nation has lost President Harding. The world knew his kindness and his humanity, his greatness and his character. He has left his mark upon history. He has made justice more certain and peace more secure. The surpassing tribute paid to his memory as he was borne across the continent to rest at last at home revealed the place lie held in the hearts of the American people [...]

[...]It is our duty, under the inspiration of his example, to take up the burdens which he was permitted to lay down, and to develop and support the wise principles of government which he represented.

For us peace reigns everywhere. We desire to perpetuate it always by granting full justice to others and requiring of others full justice to ourselves.

Our country has one cardinal principle to maintain in its foreign policy. It is an American principle. It must be an American policy. We attend to our own affairs, conserve our own strength, and protect the interests of our own citizens; but we recognize thoroughly our obligation to help others, reserving to the decision of our own judgment the time, the place, and the method. We realize the common bond of humanity. We know the inescapable law of service.

Our country has definitely refused to adopt and ratify the covenant of the League of Nations. We have not felt warranted in assuming the responsibilities which its members have assumed. I am not proposing any change in this policy; neither is the Senate. The incident, so far as we are concerned, is closed. The League exists as a foreign agency. We hope it will be helpful. But the United States sees no reason to limit its own freedom and independence of action by joining it. We shall do well to recognize this basic fact in all national affairs and govern ourselves accordingly [...]

Pending before the Senate is a proposal that this government give its support to the Permanent Court of International Justice, which is a new and somewhat different plan. This is not a partisan question. It should not assume an artificial importance. The court is merely a convenient instrument of adjustment to which we could go, but to which we could not be brought. It should be discussed with entire candor, not by a political but by a judicial method, without pressure and without prejudice. Partisanship has no place in our foreign relations. As I wish to see a court established, and as the proposal presents the only practical plan on which many nations have ever agreed, though it may not meet every desire, I therefore commend it to the favorable consideration of the Senate, with the proposed reservations clearly indicating our refusal to adhere to the League of Nations [...]

The world has had enough of the curse of hatred and selfishness, of destruction and war. It has had enough of the wrongful use of material power. For the healing of the nations there must be good will and charity, confidence and peace. The time has come for a more practical use of moral power, and more reliance upon the principle that right makes its own might. Our authority among the nations must be represented by justice and mercy. It is necessary not only to have faith, but to make sacrifices for our faith. The spiritual forces of the world make all its final determinations. It is with these voices that America should speak. Whenever they declare a righteous purpose there need be no doubt that they will be heard. America has taken her place in the world as a Republic – free, independent, powerful. The best service that can be rendered to humanity is the assurance that this place will be maintained.

Herbert Hoover

1874–1964
31st President: March 4, 1929–March 4, 1933

In the early days of the Great Depression, ordinary Americans and their leaders hoped that the crisis was temporary, and the bullish success of the 1920s could be regained and pursued to ever greater heights in the 1930s.

The government's fight-back began with voluntary measures, such as calls to businesses not to cut wages or fire workers, but the economic situation left employers with little choice. Later moves saw a shift away from the ideal of small government to measures like large state construction projects to provide employment. The Hoover administration's final attempt at economic stimulation was the creation of the Reconstruction Finance Corporation in July 1932, a Federal agency with the authority to lend up to $2billion to banks. But this sum was not large enough, the bank failures continued, and Hoover was voted out of office in March 1933, as U.S. unemployment hit 25%. The pessimism and fear to which Hoover refers to in his speech were far from unwarranted; the Great Depression was to last until 1941.

The country has enjoyed a large degree of prosperity and sound progress during the past year with a steady improvement in methods of production and distribution and consequent advancement in standards of living. Progress has, of course, been unequal among industries, and some, such as coal, lumber, leather, and textiles, still lag behind. The long upward trend of fundamental progress, however, gave rise to over-optimism as to profits, which translated itself into a wave of uncontrolled speculation in securities, resulting in the diversion of capital from business to the stock market and the inevitable crash. The natural consequences have been a reduction in the consumption of luxuries and semi-necessities by those who have met with losses, and a number of persons thrown temporarily out of employment. Prices of agricultural products dealt in upon the great markets have been affected in sympathy with the stock crash.

Fortunately, the Federal reserve system had taken measures to strengthen the position against the day when speculation would break, which together with the strong position of the banks has carried the whole credit system through the crisis without impairment. The capital which has been hitherto absorbed in stock-market loans for speculative purposes is now returning to the normal channels of business. There has been no inflation in the prices of commodities; there has been no undue accumulation of goods, and foreign trade has expanded to a magnitude which exerts a steadying influence upon activity in industry and employment.

The sudden threat of unemployment and especially the recollection of the economic consequences of previous crashes under a much less secured financial system created unwarranted pessimism and fear. It was recalled that past storms of similar character had resulted in retrenchment of construction, reduction of wages, and laying off of workers. The natural result was the tendency of business agencies throughout the country to pause in their plans and proposals for continuation and extension of their businesses, and this hesitation unchecked could in itself intensify into a depression with widespread unemployment and suffering.

I have, therefore, instituted systematic, voluntary measures of cooperation with the business institutions and with State and municipal authorities to make certain that fundamental businesses of the country shall continue as usual, that wages and therefore consuming power shall not be reduced, and that a special effort shall be made to expand construction work in order to assist in equalizing other deficits in employment. Due to the enlarged sense of cooperation and responsibility which has grown in the business world during the past few years the response has been remarkable and satisfactory. We have canvassed the Federal Government and

151

instituted measures of prudent expansion in such work that should be helpful, and upon which the different departments will make some early recommendations to Congress.

I am convinced that through these measures we have reestablished confidence. Wages should remain stable. A very large degree of industrial unemployment and suffering which would otherwise have occurred has been prevented. Agricultural prices have reflected the returning confidence. The measures taken must be vigorously pursued until normal conditions are restored.

Franklin D. Roosevelt

1882–1945
32nd President: March 4, 1933–April 12, 1945

Over the course of 1940, the Nazi occupation of Europe proceeded with seeming inexorability. America's existing policy of neutrality came to seem increasingly untenable, and President Franklin D. Roosevelt sought to persuade Congress and the country to support an interventionist role in the troubles of the old world. In the "Four Freedoms" speech, he argued that people in all nations deserve freedom of speech, the freedom to worship God in a way of their choosing, freedom from want, and freedom from fear. Armed defense of democratic existence was being waged throughout the world, he said, and it was time for the U.S.A. to bring its great strength to the fight.

Armed defense of democratic existence is now being gallantly waged in four continents. If that defense fails, all the population and all the resources of Europe and Asia and Africa and Australasia will be dominated by conquerors and let us remember that the total of those populations and their resources in those four continents greatly exceeds the sum total of the population and the resources of the whole of the Western Hemisphere – many times over.

In times like these it is immature – and incidentally, untrue – for anybody to brag that an unprepared America, single-handed, and with one hand tied behind its back, can hold off the whole world.

No realistic American can expect from a dictator's peace international generosity, or return of true independence, or world disarmament, or freedom of expression, or freedom of religion – or even good business.

Such a peace would bring no security for us or for our neighbors. "Those, who would give up essential liberty to purchase a little temporary safety, deserve neither liberty nor safety."

As a nation, we may take pride in the fact that we are softhearted; but we cannot afford to be soft-headed.

We must always be wary of those who with sounding brass and a tinkling cymbal preach the "ism" of appeasement.

We must especially beware of that small group of selfish men who would clip the wings of the American eagle in order to feather their own nests.
I have recently pointed out how quickly the tempo of modern warfare could bring into our very midst the physical attack which we must eventually expect if the dictator nations win this war.

There is much loose talk of our immunity from immediate and direct invasion from across the seas. Obviously, as long as the British Navy retains its power, no such danger exists. Even if there were no British Navy, it is not probable that any enemy would be stupid enough to attack us by landing troops in the United States from across thousands of miles of ocean, until it had acquired strategic bases from which to operate.

But we learn much from the lessons of the past years in Europe – particularly the lesson of Norway, whose essential seaports were captured by treachery and surprise built up over a series of years.

The first phase of the invasion of this Hemisphere would not be the landing of regular troops. The necessary strategic points would be occupied by secret agents and by their dupes – and great numbers of them are already here, and in Latin America. As long as the aggressor nations maintain the offensive, they – not we – will choose the time and the place and the method of their attack.

That is why the future of all the American Republics is today in serious danger.

That is why this Annual Message to the Congress is unique in our history.

That is why every member of the Executive Branch of the Government and every member of the Congress face great responsibility; great accountability.

The need of the moment is that our actions and our policy should be devoted primarily – almost exclusively – to meeting this foreign peril. For all our domestic problems are now a part of the great emergency.

Just as our national policy in internal affairs has been based upon a decent respect for the rights and the dignity of all of our fellow men within our gates, so our national policy in foreign affairs has been based on a decent respect for the rights and the dignity of all nations, large and small. And the justice of morality must and will win in the end.

Jimmy Carter

1924
39th President: January 20, 1977–January 20, 1981

President Jimmy Carter gave his first State of the Union Address at a time when the U.S. economy was stagnant. Dependency on oil imports was just as high as it had been during the oil crisis, he was already having problems with Congress over the domestic budget, and, although there had been a reduction in unemployment, there were rumblings of discontent that more had not been achieved in the first year of his presidency. What he made clear was his belief that without the will and hard work of the people, nothing any government did would get the country's economy back on track.

There is all across our land a growing sense of peace and a sense of common purpose. This sense of unity cannot be expressed in programs or in legislation or in dollars. It's an achievement that belongs to every individual American. This unity ties together, and it towers over all our efforts here in Washington, and it serves as an inspiring beacon for all of us who are elected to serve.

This new atmosphere demands a new spirit, a partnership between those of us who lead and those who elect. The foundations of this partnership are truth, the courage to face hard decisions, concern for one another and the common good over special interests, and a basic faith and trust in the wisdom and strength and judgment of the American people.

For the first time in a generation, we are not haunted by a major international crisis or by domestic turmoil, and we now have a rare and a priceless opportunity to address persistent problems and burdens which come to us as a nation, quietly and steadily getting worse over the years [...]

We must make a maximum effort, because if we do not aim for the best, we are very likely to achieve little. I see no benefit to the country if we delay, because the problems will only get worse [...]

We here in Washington must move away from crisis management, and we must establish clear goals for the future, immediate and the distant future, which will let us work together and not in conflict. Never again should we neglect a growing crisis like the shortage of energy, where further delay will only lead to more harsh and painful solutions.

Every day we spend more than $120 million for foreign oil. This slows our economic growth, it lowers the value of the dollar overseas, and it aggravates unemployment and inflation here at home.

Now we know what we must do, increase production. We must cut down on waste. And we must use more of those fuels which are plentiful and more permanent. We must be fair to people, and we must not disrupt our Nation's economy and our budget [...]

Our main task at home this year, with energy a central element, is the Nation's economy. We must continue the recovery and further cut unemployment and inflation.

Last year was a good one for the United States. We reached all of our major economic goals for 1977. Four million new jobs were created, an alltime record, and the number of unemployed dropped by more than a million. Unemployment right now is the lowest it has been since 1974, and not since World War II has such a high percentage of American people been employed.

The rate of inflation went down. There was a good growth in business profits and investments, the source of more jobs for our workers, and a higher standard of living for all our people. After taxes and inflation, there was a healthy increase in workers' wages.

And this year, our country will have the first $2 trillion economy in the history of the world. Now, we are proud of this progress the first year, but we must do even better in the future.

We still have serious problems on which all of us must work together. Our trade deficit is too large. Inflation is still too high, and too many Americans still do not have a job.

Now, I didn't have any simple answers for all these problems. But we have developed an economic policy that is working, because it's simple, balanced, and fair. It's based on four principles: First, the economy must keep on expanding to produce new jobs and better income, which our people need. The fruits of growth must be widely shared. More jobs must be made available to those who have been bypassed until now. And the tax system must be made fairer and simpler.

Secondly, private business and not the Government must lead the expansion in the future.

Third, we must lower the rate of inflation and keep it down. Inflation slows down economic growth, and it's the most cruel to the poor and also to the elderly and others who live on fixed incomes.

And fourth, we must contribute to the strength of the world economy [...]

I'll be asking you for a substantial increase in funds for public jobs for our young people, and I also am recommending that the Congress continue the public service employment programs at more than twice the level of a year ago. When welfare reform is completed, we will have more than a million additional jobs so that those on welfare who are able to work can work.

However, again, we know that in our free society, private business is still the best source of new jobs. Therefore, I will propose a new program to encourage businesses to hire young and disadvantaged Americans. These young people only need skills and a chance in order to take their place in our economic system. Let's give them the chance they need. A major step in the right direction would be the early passage of a greatly improved Humphrey–Hawkins Bill [...]

Economic success at home is also the key to success in our international economic policy. An effective energy program, strong investment and productivity, and controlled inflation will improve our trade balance and balance it, and it will help to protect the integrity of the dollar overseas.

By working closely with our friends abroad, we can promote the economic health of the whole world, with fair and balanced agreements lowering the barriers to trade.

Despite the inevitable pressures that build up when the world economy suffers from high unemployment, we must firmly resist the demands for self-defeating protectionism. But free trade must also be fair trade. And I am determined to protect American industry and American workers against foreign trade practices which are unfair or illegal […]

During these past years, Americans have seen our Government grow far from us. For some citizens, the Government has almost become like a foreign country, so strange and distant that we've often had to deal with it through trained ambassadors who have sometimes become too powerful and too influential, lawyers, accountants, and lobbyists. This cannot go on.

We must have what Abraham Lincoln wanted, a government for the people. We've made progress toward that kind of government. You've given me the authority I requested to reorganize the Federal bureaucracy. And I am using that authority […]

But even the best organized Government will only be as effective as the people who carry out its policies. For this reason, I consider civil service reform to be absolutely vital. Worked out with the civil servants themselves, this reorganization plan will restore the merit principle to a system which has grown into a bureaucratic maze. It will provide greater management flexibility and better rewards for better performance without compromising job security.

Then and only then can we have a government that is efficient, open, and truly worthy of our people's understanding and respect. I have promised that we will have such a government, and I intend to keep that promise.

In our foreign policy, the separation of people from government has been in the past a source of weakness and error. In a democratic system like ours, foreign policy decisions must be able to stand the test of public examination and public debate.

If we make a mistake in this administration, it will be on the side of frankness and openness with the American people.

In our modern world, when the deaths of literally millions of people can result from a few terrifying seconds of destruction, the path of national strength and security is identical to the path of peace.

Tonight, I am happy to report that because we are strong, our Nation is at peace with the world.

We are a confident nation. We've restored a moral basis for our foreign policy. The very heart of our identity as a nation is our firm commitment to human rights.

We stand for human rights because we believe that government has as a purpose to promote the well-being of its citizens. This is true in our domestic policy; it's also true in our foreign policy. The world must know that in support of human rights, the United States will stand firm.

We expect no quick or easy results, but there has been significant movement toward greater freedom and humanity in several parts of the world.

Thousands of political prisoners have been freed. The leaders of the world, even our ideological adversaries, now see that their attitude toward fundamental human rights affects their standing in the international community, and it affects their relations with the United States.

To serve the interests of every American, our foreign policy has three major goals. The first and prime concern is and will remain the security of our country [...]

Every American has a stake in our second major goal, a world at peace. In a nuclear age, each of us is threatened when peace is not secured everywhere. We are trying to promote harmony in those parts of the world where major differences exist among other nations and threaten international peace.

In the Middle East, we are contributing our good offices to maintain the momentum of the current negotiations and to keep open the lines of communication among the Middle Eastern leaders. The whole world has a great stake in the success of these efforts. This is a precious opportunity for a historic settlement of a longstanding conflict, an opportunity which may never come again in our lifetime.

Our role has been difficult and sometimes thankless and controversial. But it has been constructive and it has been necessary, and it will continue.

Our third major foreign-policy goal is one that touches the life of every American citizen every day, world economic growth and stability.

This requires strong economic performance by the industrialized democracies like ourselves and progress in resolving the global energy crisis. Last fall, with the help of others, we succeeded in our vigorous efforts to maintain the stability of the price of oil. But as many foreign leaders have emphasized to me personally and, I am sure, to you, the greatest future contribution that America can make to the world economy would be an effective energy conservation program here at home. We will not hesitate to take the actions needed to protect the integrity of the American dollar.

We are trying to develop a more just international system. And in this spirit, we are supporting the struggle for human development in Africa, in Asia, and in Latin America [...]

It has been said that our best years are behind us. But I say again that America's best is still ahead. We have emerged from bitter experiences chastened but proud, confident once again, ready to face challenges once again, and united once again [...]

Our task, to use the words of Senator Humphrey, is "reconciliation, rebuilding, and rebirth."

Reconciliation of private needs and interests into a higher purpose.

Rebuilding the old dreams of justice and liberty, and country and community.

Rebirth of our faith in the common good.

Each of us here tonight, and all who are listening in your homes, must rededicate ourselves to serving the common good. We are a community, a beloved community, all of us. Our individual fates are linked, our futures intertwined. And if we act in that knowledge and in that spirit, together, as the Bible says, we can move mountains.

Barack Obama

1961
44th President: January 20, 2009–January 20, 2017

President Barack Obama used his final State of the Union address to send a firm message of support to ordinary working Americans who were continuing to suffer the effects of the 2008 financial crisis. However, media commentators were quick to point out that, in 2008, his administration had bailed out the bankers to the tune of $700 billion, and in February 2014, Obama had signed a Bill that would cut food stamps by $8.7 billion. The speech was both praised for its pithy rhetoric and criticized for picking an obvious target in the banks.

I believe a thriving private sector is the lifeblood of our economy. I think there are outdated regulations that need to be changed, and there's red tape that needs to be cut. But after years of record corporate profits, working families won't get more opportunity or bigger paychecks by letting big banks or big oil or hedge funds make their own rules at the expense of everyone else; or by allowing attacks on collective bargaining to go unanswered. Food Stamp recipients didn't cause the financial crisis; recklessness on Wall Street did. Immigrants aren't the reason wages haven't gone up enough; those decisions are made in the boardrooms that too often put quarterly earnings over long-term returns. It's sure not the average family watching tonight that avoids paying taxes through offshore accounts. In this new economy, workers and start-ups and small businesses need more of a voice, not less.

Donald Trump

1946
45th President: January 20, 2017–present

Donald Trump is arguably the most controversial U.S. president in history. At the time of writing, he has been in power for a year, and addresses the nation more often through tweets than through formal speeches. His 2018 State of the Union address was an expression of his touchstone policy of "make America great again."

[...] Americans fill the world with art and music. They push the bounds of science and discovery. And they forever remind us of what we should never forget: The people dreamed this country. The people built this country. And it is the people who are making America great again.

As long as we are proud of who we are, and what we are fighting for, there is nothing we cannot achieve.

As long as we have confidence in our values, faith in our citizens, and trust in our God, we will not fail.

Our families will thrive.

Our people will prosper.

And our Nation will forever be safe and strong and proud and mighty and free.

Thank you, and God bless America.

FAREWELL ADDRESSES

—————— ≈ ——————

George Washington

——————•——————

1732–1799
1st President: April 30, 1789–March 4, 1797

President George Washington's Farewell Address was written in the form of a speech, but never actually delivered. In its 51 paragraphs, he states his reasons for not seeking another term as president and lays out his vision for the country that had so recently been united to gain its independence. He discusses the need for vigilance against creeping infringements on national and individual liberty, expresses his opinion that the nation is better as a unified whole and warns against both deviance from the principles laid out in the Constitution and any rebellion. He advises against bringing political parties into governance, permanent antipathy against or alliances with any particular nation, and counsels the need for morality in government.

The period for a new election of a citizen, to administer the executive government of the United States, being not far distant, and the time actually arrived, when your thoughts must be employed designating the person, who is to be clothed with that important trust, it appears to me proper, especially as it may conduce to a more distinct expression of the public voice, that I should now apprize you of the resolution I have formed, to decline being considered among the number of those out of whom a choice is to be made […]

The acceptance of, and continuance hitherto in, the office to which your suffrages have twice called me, have been a uniform sacrifice of inclination to the opinion of duty, and to a deference for what appeared to be your desire. I constantly hoped, that it would have been much earlier in my power, consistently with motives, which I was not at liberty to disregard, to return to that retirement, from which I had been reluctantly drawn. The strength of my inclination to do this, previous to the last election, had even led to the preparation of an address to declare it to you; but mature reflection on the then perplexed and critical posture of our affairs with foreign nations, and the unanimous advice of persons entitled to my confidence impelled me to abandon the idea [...]

The impressions, with which I first undertook the arduous trust, were explained on the proper occasion. In the discharge of this trust, I will only say, that I have, with good intentions, contributed towards the organization and administration of the government the best exertions of which a very fallible judgment was capable. Not unconscious, in the outset, of the inferiority of my qualifications, experience in my own eyes, perhaps still more in the eyes of others, has strengthened the motives to diffidence of myself; and every day the increasing weight of years admonishes me more and more, that the shade of retirement is as necessary to me as it will be welcome. Satisfied, that, if any circumstances have given peculiar value to my services, they were temporary, I have the consolation to believe, that, while choice and prudence invite me to quit the political scene, patriotism does not forbid it.

In looking forward to the moment, which is intended to terminate the career of my public life, my feelings do not permit me to suspend the deep acknowledgment of that debt of gratitude, which I owe to my beloved country for the many honors it has conferred upon me; still more for the steadfast confidence with which it has supported me; and for the opportunities I have thence enjoyed of manifesting my inviolable attachment, by services faithful and persevering, though in usefulness unequal to my zeal. If benefits have resulted to our country from these services, let it always be remembered to your praise, and as an instructive example in our annals, that under circumstances in which the passions, agitated in every direction, were liable to mislead, amidst appearances sometimes dubious, vicissitudes of fortune often discouraging, in situations in which not unfrequently want of success has countenanced the spirit of criticism, the constancy of your support was the essential prop of the efforts, and a guarantee of the plans by which they were effected [...]

Though, in reviewing the incidents of my administration, I am unconscious of intentional error, I am nevertheless too sensible of my defects not to think it probable that I may have committed many errors. Whatever they may be, I fervently beseech the Almighty to avert or mitigate the evils to which they may tend. I shall also carry with me the hope, that my Country will never cease to view them with indulgence; and that, after 45 years of my life dedicated to its service with an upright zeal, the faults of incompetent abilities will be consigned to oblivion, as myself must soon be to the mansions of rest.

Relying on its kindness in this as in other things, and actuated by that fervent love toward it, which is so natural to a man, who views it in the native soil of himself and his progenitors for several generations; I anticipate with pleasing expectation that retreat, in which I promise myself to realize, without alloy, the sweet enjoyment of partaking, in the midst of my fellow-citizens, the benign influence of good laws under a free government, the ever favorite object of my heart, and the happy reward, as I trust, of our mutual cares, labors, and dangers.

Dwight D. Eisenhower

1890–1969
34th President: January 20, 1953–January 20, 1961

At the end of his eight-year term in the Oval Office, President Dwight D. Eisenhower addressed the American people, looking both back on his achievements and toward America's and the world's future, with reference to the U.S.S.R.. A major part of the speech is taken up with the increase in size of the U.S. military, which he believed was a necessity, whilst warning against the possibility of the "military–industrial complex" becoming over-powerful, whether by intent or accident, fearing that the peaceful methods and goals of the majority of Americans would be subsumed, and that the liberty that they held dear would be lost in the name of national security and the interests of the armaments industry or the scientific elite.

Good evening, my fellow Americans.

[…] Three days from now, after half century in the service of our country, I shall lay down the responsibilities of office as, in traditional and solemn ceremony, the authority of the Presidency is vested in my successor. This evening, I come to you with a message of leave-taking and farewell, and to share a few final thoughts with you, my countrymen […]

We now stand ten years past the midpoint of a century that has witnessed four major wars among great nations. Three of these involved our own country. Despite these holocausts, America is today the strongest, the most influential, and most productive nation in the world. Understandably proud of this pre-eminence, we yet realize that America's leadership and prestige depend, not merely upon our unmatched material progress, riches, and military strength, but on how we use our power in the interests of world peace and human betterment.

Throughout America's adventure in free government, our basic purposes have been to keep the peace, to foster progress in human achievement, and to enhance liberty, dignity, and integrity among peoples and among nations. To strive for less would be unworthy of a free and religious people. Any failure traceable to arrogance, or our lack of comprehension, or readiness to sacrifice would inflict upon us grievous hurt, both at home and abroad [...]

Crises there will continue to be. In meeting them, whether foreign or domestic, great or small, there is a recurring temptation to feel that some spectacular and costly action could become the miraculous solution to all current difficulties. A huge increase in newer elements of our defenses; development of unrealistic programs to cure every ill in agriculture; a dramatic expansion in basic and applied research – these and many other possibilities, each possibly promising in itself, may be suggested as the only way to the road we wish to travel.

But each proposal must be weighed in the light of a broader consideration: The need to maintain balance in and among national programs, balance between the private and the public economy, balance between the cost and hoped for advantages, balance between the clearly necessary and the comfortably desirable, balance between our essential requirements as a nation and the duties imposed by the nation upon the individual, balance between actions of the moment and the national welfare of the future. Good judgment seeks balance and progress. Lack of it eventually finds imbalance and frustration. The record of many decades stands as proof that our people and their Government have, in the main, understood these truths and have responded to them well, in the face of threat and stress [...]

A vital element in keeping the peace is our military establishment. Our arms must be mighty, ready for instant action, so that no potential aggressor may be tempted to risk his own destruction. Our military organization today bears little relation to that known of any of my predecessors in peacetime, or, indeed, by the fighting men of World War II or Korea.

Until the latest of our world conflicts, the United States had no armaments industry. American makers of plowshares could, with time and as required, make swords as well. But we can no longer risk emergency improvisation of national defense. We have been compelled to create a permanent armaments industry of vast proportions.

Added to this, three and a half million men and women are directly engaged in the defence establishment. We annually spend on military security alone more than the net income of all United States cooperations – corporations [...]

In the councils of government, we must guard against the acquisition of unwarranted influence, whether sought or unsought, by the military–industrial complex. The potential for the disastrous rise of misplaced power exists and will persist. We must never let the weight of this combination endanger our liberties or democratic processes. We should take nothing for granted. Only an alert and knowledgeable citizenry can compel the proper meshing of the huge industrial and military machinery of defense with our peaceful methods and goals, so that security and liberty may prosper together [...]

Another factor in maintaining balance involves the element of time. As we peer into society's future, we – you and I, and our government – must avoid the impulse to live only for today, plundering for our own ease and convenience the precious resources of tomorrow. We cannot mortgage the material assets of our grandchildren without risking the loss also of their political and spiritual heritage. We want democracy to survive for all generations to come, not to become the insolvent phantom of tomorrow.

During the long lane of the history yet to be written, America knows that this world of ours, ever growing smaller, must avoid becoming a community of dreadful fear and hate, and be, instead, a proud confederation of mutual trust and respect. Such a confederation must be one of equals. The weakest must come to the conference table with the same confidence as do we, protected as we are by our moral, economic, and military strength. That table, though scarred by many past frustrations – past frustrations, cannot be abandoned for the certain agony of disarmament – of the battlefield [...]

So, in this, my last goodnight to you as your President, I thank you for the many opportunities you have given me for public service in war and in peace. I trust that in that service you find some things worthy. As for the rest of it, I know you will find ways to improve performance in the future.

You and I, my fellow citizens, need to be strong in our faith that all nations, under God, will reach the goal of peace with justice. May we be ever unswerving in devotion to principle, confident but humble with power, diligent in pursuit of the Nation's great goals.

To all the peoples of the world, I once more give expression to America's prayerful and continuing aspiration: We pray that peoples of all faiths, all races, all nations, may have their great human needs satisfied; that those now denied opportunity shall come to enjoy it to the full; that all who yearn for freedom may experience its few spiritual blessings. Those who have freedom will understand, also, its heavy responsibility; that all who are insensitive to the needs of others will learn charity; and that the sources – scourges of poverty, disease, and ignorance will be made [to] disappear from the earth; and that in the goodness of time, all peoples will come to live together in a peace guaranteed by the binding force of mutual respect and love.

Now, on Friday noon, I am to become a private citizen. I am proud to do so. I look forward to it.

Thank you, and good night.

Richard Nixon

1913–1994
37th President: January 20, 1969–August 9, 1974

On August 8, 1974, President Richard Nixon announced his resignation to the nation to avoid impeachment for his role in the Watergate scandal. During the 1972 presidential election campaign, five men had been caught breaking into the Democratic Party HQ in the Watergate Hotel, Washington. An informant from the FBI – "Deep Throat" – passed on the information to Washington Post *reporters Carl Bernstein and Bob Woodward that the men had links to the Nixon White House. It emerged that tapes of the President's conversations from the relevant period had been wiped, perhaps deliberately, and the Democrat-controlled House Judiciary Committee began impeachment proceedings. When the Supreme Court ruled that the remaining White House tapes should be released to the Special Prosecutor, the game was up. The "Smoking Gun" tape, released on August 5, made it obvious that the President had known about the plot from the beginning and had actively tried to stop the FBI investigation. Four days later, he resigned.*

Good evening. This is the thirty-seventh time I have spoken to you from this office, where so many decisions have been made that shaped the history of this Nation. Each time I have done so to discuss with you some matter that I believe affected the national interest [...]

In the past few days, however, it has become evident to me that I no longer have a strong enough political base in the Congress to justify continuing that effort. As long as there was such a base, I felt strongly that it was necessary to see the constitutional process through to its conclusion, that to do otherwise would be unfaithful to the spirit of that deliberately difficult process and a dangerously destabilizing precedent for the future.

From the discussions I have had with Congressional and other leaders, I have concluded that because of the Watergate matter I might not have the support of the Congress that I would consider necessary to back the very difficult decisions and carry out the duties of this office in the way the interests of the nation would require. I have never been a quitter. To leave office before my term is completed is abhorrent to every instinct in my body. But as President, I must put the interest of America first. America needs a full-time President and a full-time Congress, particularly at this time with problems we face at home and abroad [...]

Therefore, I shall resign the Presidency effective at noon tomorrow. Vice President Ford will be sworn in as President at that hour in this office.

As I recall the high hopes for America with which we began this second term, I feel a great sadness that I will not be here in this office working on your behalf to achieve those hopes in the next two-and-a-half years. But in turning over direction of the Government to Vice President Ford, I know, as I told the Nation when I nominated him for that office 10 months ago, that the leadership of America will be in good hands.

In passing this office to the Vice President, I also do so with the profound sense of the weight of responsibility that will fall on his shoulders tomorrow and, therefore, of the understanding, the patience, the cooperation he will need from all Americans.

As he assumes that responsibility, he will deserve the help and the support of all of us. As we look to the future, the first essential is to begin healing the wounds of this Nation, to put the bitterness and divisions of the recent past behind us, and to rediscover those shared ideals that lie at the heart of our strength and unity as a great and as a free people […]

I regret deeply any injuries that may have been done in the course of the events that led to this decision. I would say only that if some of my judgments were wrong, and some were wrong, they were made in what I believed at the time to be the best interest of the Nation.

To those who have stood with me during these past difficult months, to my family, my friends, to many others who joined in supporting my cause because they believed it was right, I will be eternally grateful for your support […]

Sometimes I have succeeded and sometimes I have failed, but always I have taken heart from what Theodore Roosevelt once said about the man in the arena, "whose face is marred by dust and sweat and blood, who strives valiantly, who errs and comes short again and again because there is not effort without error and shortcoming, but who does actually strive to do the deed, who knows the great enthusiasms, the great devotions, who spends himself in a worthy cause, who at the best knows in the end the triumphs of high achievements and who at the worst, if he fails, at least fails while daring greatly." I pledge to you tonight that as long as I have a breath of life in my body, I shall continue in that spirit. I shall continue to work for the great causes to which I have been dedicated throughout my years as a Congressman, a Senator, a Vice President, and President, the cause of peace not just for America but among all nations, prosperity, justice, and opportunity for all of our people.

There is one cause above all to which I have been devoted and to which I shall always be devoted for as long as I live.

When I first took the oath of office as President five-and-a-half years ago, I made this sacred commitment to "consecrate my office, my energies, and all the wisdom I can summon to the cause of peace among nations."

I have done my very best in all the days since to be true to that pledge. As a result of these efforts, I am confident that the world is a safer place today, not only for the people of America but for the people of all nations, and that all of our children have a better chance than before of living in peace rather than dying in war.

This, more than anything, is what I hoped to achieve when I sought the Presidency.

This, more than anything, is what I hope will be my legacy to you, to our country, as I leave the Presidency. To have served in this office is to have felt a very personal sense of kinship with each and every American. In leaving it, I do so with this prayer: May God's grace be with you in all the days ahead.

MISCELLANEOUS

"SWING AROUND THE CIRCLE" SPEECH TOUR

Andrew Johnson

1808–1875
17th President: April 15, 1865–March 4, 1869

Vice President Andrew Johnson, who according to witnesses was drunk at the second inauguration of Abraham Lincoln, unexpectedly became president when Lincoln was assassinated just a month later, in April 1865. Johnson was a controversial and vitriolic leader, who in August and September of 1866 embarked on a speaking tour called the Swing around the Circle in an attempt to win support for his post-Civil War Reconstruction policies. Initially, he received favorable press, but as the tour went on, he encountered worse and worse heckling, to which he responded in kind, eventually, in Cleveland, speaking a memorable line that was quoted across the press to the destruction of Johnson's credibility.

I don't care about my dignity.

MESSAGE TO CONGRESS REGARDING ENVIRONMENTAL PRESERVATION

William Taft

1857–1930

27th President: March 4, 1909–March 4, 1913

In the early days of settlement, the lands of the North American continent seemed virtually endless. But a hundred years ago, politicians were beginning to face the reality that this was not so. In the Oregon land fraud scandal of the early 1900s, government land grants were illegally obtained with the connivance of officials, and came into the control of owners who cared little for it other than as a resource, especially of timber. That timber was in large part giant sequoias and giant redwoods – the tallest and most awe-inspiring trees in the world. Ninety-five percent of the country's giant redwoods were cut down by loggers, with the remaining five percent now surviving in national parks.

In 1860, we had a public domain of 1,055,911,288 acres. We have now 731,354,081 acres, confined largely to the mountain ranges and the arid and semiarid plains. We have, in addition, 368,035,975 acres of land in Alaska.

The public lands were, during the earliest administrations, treated as a national asset for the liquidation of the public debt and as a source of reward for our soldiers and sailors. Later on they were donated in large amounts in aid of the construction of wagon roads and railways, in order to open up regions in the West then almost inaccessible. All the principal land statutes were enacted more than a quarter of a century ago. The Homestead Act, the preemption and timber-culture act, the coal land and the mining acts were among these. The rapid disposition of the public lands under the early statutes, and the lax methods of distribution prevailing, due, I think, to the belief that these lands should rapidly pass into private ownership, gave rise to the impression that the public domain was legitimate prey for the unscrupulous, and that it was not contrary to good morals to circumvent the land laws. This prodigal manner of disposition resulted in the passing of large areas of valuable land and many of our national resources into the hands of persons who felt little or no responsibility for promoting the national welfare through their development. The truth is that title to millions of acres of public lands was fraudulently obtained, and that the right to recover a large part of such lands for the Government long since ceased by reason of statutes of limitations.

There has developed in recent years a deep concern in the public mind respecting the preservation and proper use of our national resources. This has been particularly directed toward the conservation of the resources of the public domain. The problem is how to save and how to utilize, how to conserve and still develop; for no sane person can contend that it is for the common good that Nature's blessings are only for unborn generations.

Among the most noteworthy reforms initiated by my distinguished predecessor were the vigorous prosecution of land frauds and the bringing to public attention of the necessity for preserving the remaining public domain from further spoliation, for the maintenance and extension of our forest resources, and for the enactment of laws amending the obsolete statutes so as to retain governmental control over that part of the public domain in which there are valuable deposits of coal, of oil, and of phosphate, and, in addition thereto, to preserve control, under conditions favorable to the public, of the lands along the streams in which the fall of water can be made to generate power to be transmitted in the form of electricity many miles to the point of its use, known as "water-power" sites.

The investigations into violations of the public land laws and the prosecution of land frauds have been vigorously continued under my administration, as has been the withdrawal of coal lands for classification and valuation and the temporary withholding of power sites.

Since March 4, 1909, temporary withdrawals of power sites have been made on 102 streams and these withdrawals therefore cover 229 percent more streams than were covered by the withdrawals made prior to that date.

MILWAUKEE ADDRESS

Theodore Roosevelt

1858–1919
26th President: September 14, 1901–March 4, 1909

The campaign speech given by presidential candidate Theodore Roosevelt in Milwaukee was not expected to be an historic occasion. Nor in the event was it a particularly fine piece of rhetoric. It is remarkable for other reasons: Roosevelt delivered it five minutes after being shot, and after the fifty-page manuscript itself had physically saved his life, being in his breast pocket along with a glasses case, hindering the passage of the bullet so that it did not pierce his heart. Roosevelt went on to give the entire ninety-minute speech before medical attention. The would-be assassin, John Flammang Schrank, claimed that the ghost of the late President William McKinley had told him to commit the act because Roosevelt was seeking a third term in office.

Eventually, in 1947, the Twenty-Second Amendment was added to the Constitution, barring presidents from serving for more than two terms. The ghost of William McKinley is not known to have offered comment.

Friends, I shall ask you to be as quiet as possible. I don't know whether you fully understand that I have just been shot; but it takes more than that to kill a Bull Moose. But fortunately I had my manuscript, so you see I was going to make a long speech, and there is a bullet - there is where the bullet went through - and it probably saved me from it going into my heart. The bullet is in me now, so that I cannot make a very long speech, but I will try my best.

And now, friends, I want to take advantage of this incident to say a word of solemn warning to my fellow countrymen. First of all, I want to say this about myself: I have altogether too important things to think of to feel any concern over my own death; and now I cannot speak to you insincerely within five minutes of being shot. I am telling you the literal truth when I say that my concern is for many other things. It is not in the least for my own life. I want you to understand that I am ahead of the game, anyway. No man has had a happier life than I have led; a happier life in every way. I have been able to do certain things that I greatly wished to do, and I am interested in doing other things. I can tell you with absolute truthfulness that I am very much uninterested in whether I am shot or not. It was just as when I was colonel of my regiment. I always felt that a private was to be excused for feeling at times some pangs of anxiety about his personal safety, but I cannot understand a man fit to be a colonel who can pay any heed to his personal safety when he is occupied as he ought to be with the absorbing desire to do his duty.

"BACK TO NORMALCY" SPEECH

Warren G. Harding

1865–1923

29th President: March 4, 1921–August 2, 1923

In May 1920, in the lead-up to the Republican Party nomination, Senator Harding gave several speeches. In Boston on May 14, he coined the term that would become his campaign slogan – "Back to normalcy." The postwar presidency of Woodrow Wilson had become increasingly unpopular as the economic situation remained dire. Harding campaigned on the theme of a return to a strict interpretation of the Monroe Doctrine, as well as the promotion of U.S. citizens' rights and small-government laissez-faire policies. He won by one of the largest margins ever, although by the time of his death in 1923, his popularity was waning.

There isn't anything the matter with the world's civilization except that humanity is viewing it through a vision impaired in a cataclysmal war. Poise has been disturbed and nerves have been racked, and fever has rendered men irrational; sometimes there have been draughts upon the dangerous cup of barbarity and men have wandered far from safe paths, but the human procession still marches in the right direction.

Here, in the United States, we feel the reflex, rather than the hurting wound, but we still think straight, and we mean to act straight, and mean to hold firmly to all that was ours when war involved us, and seek the higher attainments which are the only compensations that so supreme a tragedy may give mankind.

America's present need is not heroics, but healing; not nostrums, but normalcy; not revolution, but restoration; not agitation, but adjustment; not surgery, but serenity; not the dramatic, but the dispassionate; not experiment, but equipoise; not submergence in internationality, but sustainment in triumphant nationality [...]

This republic has its ample tasks. If we put an end to false economics which lure humanity to utter chaos, ours will be the commanding example of world leadership today. If we can prove a representative popular government under which a citizenship seeks what it may do for the government rather than what the government may do for individuals, we shall do more to make democracy safe for the world than all armed conflict ever recorded. The world needs to be reminded that all human ills are not curable by legislation, and that quantity of statutory enactment and excess of government offer no substitute for quality of citizenship [...]

There is no new appraisal for the supremacy of law. That is a thing surpassing and eternal. A contempt for international law wrought the supreme tragedy, contempt for our national and state laws will rend the glory of the republic, and failure to abide the proven laws of to-day's civilization will lead to temporary chaos [...]

My best judgment of America's needs is to steady down, to get squarely on our feet, to make sure of the right path. Let's get out of the fevered delirium of war, with the hallucination that all the money in the world is to be made in the madness of war and the wildness of its aftermath. Let us stop to consider that tranquility at home is more precious than peace abroad, and that both our good fortune and our eminence are dependent on the normal forward stride of all the American people [...]

Sober capital must make appeal to intoxicated wealth, and thoughtful labor must appeal to the radical who has no thought of the morrow, to effect the needed understanding. Exacted profits, because the golden stream is flooding, and pyramided wages to meet a mounting cost that must be halted, will speed us to disaster just as sure as the morrow comes, and we ought to think soberly and avoid it. We ought to dwell in the heights of good fortune for a generation to come, and I pray that we will, but we need a benediction of wholesome common sense to give us that assurance.

I pray for sober thinking in behalf of the future of America. No worthwhile republic ever went the tragic way to destruction, which did not begin the downward course through luxury of life and extravagance of living. More, the simple living and thrifty people will be the first to recover from a war's waste and all its burdens, and our people ought to be the first recovered. Herein is greater opportunity than lies in alliance, compact or super-government. It is America's chance to lead in example and prove to the world the reign of reason in representative popular government where people think who assume to rule [...]

It seems to me singularly appropriate to address this membership an additional word about production.

I believe most cordially in the home market first for the American product. There is no other way to assure our prosperity. I rejoice in our normal capacity to consume our rational, healthful consumption [...]

We have protected our home market with war's barrage. But the barrage has lifted with the passing of the war. The American people will not heed today, because world competition is not yet restored, but the morrow will soon come when the world will seek our markets and our trade balances, and we must think of America first or surrender our eminence.

The thought is not selfish. We want to share with the world in seeking becoming restoration. But peoples will trade and seek wealth in their exchanges, and every conflict in the adjustment of peace was founded on the hope of promoting trade conditions. I heard expressed, before the Foreign Relations Committee of the Senate, the aspirations of nationality and the hope of commerce to develop and expand aspiring peoples. Knowing that those two thoughts are inspiring all humanity, as they have since civilization began, I can only marvel at the American who consents to surrender either. There may be conscience, humanity and justice in both, and without them the glory of the republic is done. I want to go on, secure and unafraid, holding fast to the American inheritance and confident of the supreme American fulfillment.

PRINCIPLES AND IDEALS OF THE UNITED STATES GOVERNMENT

Herbert Hoover

1874–1964
31st President: March 4, 1929–March 4, 1933

Toward the close of the 1928 U.S. presidential campaign, Republican candidate Herbert Hoover extolled the virtues of free enterprise and "rugged individualism" as the basis of America's wealth and greatness, and campaigned for increased regulation and increased volunteerism. As Commerce Secretary, he was widely seen as presiding over the booming American economy. Less than eight months after his election, the Wall Street Crash occurred and his methods proved inadequate to counter the ensuing Great Depression.

This campaign now draws near to a close. The platforms of the two parties defining principles and offering solutions of various national problems have been presented and are being earnestly considered by our people.

After four months' debate it is not the Republican Party which finds reason for abandonment of any of the principles it has laid down or of the views it has expressed for solution of the problems before the country. The principles to which it adheres are rooted deeply in the foundations of our national life and the solutions which it proposed are based on experience with government and a consciousness that it may have the responsibility for placing those solutions into action [...]

I regret, however, to say that there has been revived in this campaign a proposal which would be a long step to the abandonment of our American system, to turn to the idea of government in business. Because we are faced with difficulty and doubt over certain national problems which we are faced – that is prohibition, farm relief and electrical power – our opponents propose that we must to some degree thrust government into these businesses and in effect adopt state socialism as a solution.

There is, therefore submitted to the American people the question – Shall we depart from the American system and start upon a new road. And I wish to emphasize this question on this occasion. I wish to make clear my position on the principles involved for they go to the very roots of American life in every act of our Government. I should like to state to you the effect of the extension of government into business upon our system of self government and our economic system. But even more important is the effect upon the average man. That is the effect on the very basis of liberty and freedom not only to those left outside the fold of expanded bureaucracy but to those embraced [...]

[...] Business progressiveness is dependent on competition. New methods and new ideas are the outgrowth of the spirit of adventure of individual initiative and of individual enterprise. Without adventure there is no progress. No government administration can rightly speculate and take risks with taxpayers' money. But even more important than this – leadership in business must be through the sheer rise of ability and character. That rise can take place only in the free atmosphere of competition. Competition is closed by bureaucracy. Certainly political choice is a feeble basis for choice of leaders to conduct a business [...]

Bureaucracy is ever desirous of spreading its influence and its power. You cannot give to a government the mastery of the daily working life of a people without at the same time giving it mastery of the peoples' souls and thoughts. Every expansion of government means that government in order to protect itself from political consequences of its errors and wrongs is driven onward and onward without peace to greater and greater control of the country's press and platform. Free speech does not live many hours after free industry and free commerce die.

It is false liberalism that interprets itself into the government operation of business. The bureaucratization of our country would poison the very roots of liberalism that is free speech, free assembly, free press, political equality and equality of opportunity. It is the road, not to more liberty, but to less liberty. Liberalism should be found not striving to spread bureaucracy, but striving to set bounds to it. True liberalism seeks freedom first in the confident belief that without freedom the pursuit of all other blessings and benefits is vain. That belief is the foundation of all American progress, political as well as economic.

Liberalism is a force truly of the spirit, a force proceeding from the deep realization that economic freedom cannot be sacrificed if political freedom is to be preserved. Even if governmental conduct of business could give us more efficiency instead of giving us decreased efficiency, the fundamental objection to it would remain unaltered and unabated. It would destroy political equality. It would cramp and cripple mental and spiritual energies of our people. It would dry up the spirit of liberty and progress. It would extinguish equality of opportunity, and for these reasons fundamentally and primarily it must be resisted. For 150 years, liberalism has found its true spirit in the American system, not in the European systems [...]

There is but one consideration in testing these proposals – that is public interest. I do not doubt the sincerity of those who advocate these methods of solving our problems. I believe they will give equal credit to our honesty. If I believed that the adoption of such proposals would decrease taxes, cure abuses or corruption, would produce better service, decrease rates or benefit employees; if I believed they would bring economic equality, would stimulate endeavor, would encourage invention and support individual initiative, would provide equality of opportunity; if I believed that these proposals would not wreck our democracy but would strengthen the foundations of social and spiritual progress in America – or if they would do a few of these things – then I would not hesitate roposals, stupendous as they are, even though such acceptance would result in the governmental operation of all our power and the buying and selling of the products of our farms or any other product. But it is not true that such benefits would result to the public. The contrary would be true [...]

As a result of our distinctly American system, our country has become the land of opportunity to those born without inheritance not merely because of the wealth of its resources and industry but because of this freedom of initiative and enterprise. Russia has natural resources equal to ours. Her people are equally industrious but she has not had the blessings of 150 years of our form of government and of our social system. The wisdom of our forefathers in their conception that progress must be the sum of the progress of free individuals has been reenforced by all of the great leaders of the country since that day. Jackson, Lincoln, Cleveland, McKinley, Roosevelt, Wilson, and Coolidge have stood unalterably for these principles. By adherence to the principles of decentralization, selfgovernment, ordered liberty, and opportunity and freedom to the individual our American experiment has yielded a degree of well-being unparalleled in all the world. It has come nearer to the abolition of poverty, to the abolition of fear of want that humanity has ever reached before. Progress of the past seven years is the proof of it. It furnishes an answer to those who would ask us to abandon the system by which this has been accomplished [...]

I wish to say something more on what I believe is the outstanding ideal in our whole political, economic and social system – that is equality of opportunity. We have carried this ideal farther into our life than has any other nation in the world. Equality of opportunity is the right of every American, rich or poor, foreign or native born, without respect to race or faith or color, to attain that position in life to which his ability and character entitle him. We must carry this ideal further than to economic and political fields alone. The first steps to equality of opportunity are that there should be no child in America that has not been born and does not live under sound conditions of health, that does not have full opportunity for education from the beginning to the end of our institutions, that is not free from injurious labor, that does not have stimulation to accomplish to the fullest of its capacities […]

Furthermore, equality of opportunity in my vision requires an equal opportunity to the people in every section of our country. In these past few years some groups in our country have lagged behind others in the march of progress. They have not had the same opportunity. I refer more particularly to those engaged in the textile, coal and in the agricultural industries. We can assist in solving these problems by cooperation of our Government. To the agricultural industry we shall need advance initial capital to assist them, to stabilize and conduct their own industry. But this proposal is that they shall conduct it themselves, not by the Government. It is in the interest of our cities that we shall bring agriculture into full stability and prosperity.

I know you will cooperate gladly in the faith that in the common prosperity of our country lies its future.

FIRST *FIRESIDE CHAT*: BANKING

Franklin D. Roosevelt

1882–1945
32nd President: March 4, 1933–April 12, 1945

The Fireside Chats *were a series of thirty radio addresses given by Franklin D. Roosevelt between 1933 and 1944. The president took an informal approach to political issues of the day, including the financial crisis and World War II, explaining the issues and the actions of his administration in unpretentious terms. Americans certainly needed the reassurance. By the early 1930s the Great Depression had truly taken hold, with the suicide rate in the country tripling between 1929 and 1933.*

The chats were a success, increasing public confidence in both the president and his policies; the day after the first of them, newspapers around the country reported queues of people waiting to put their money back into banks. The Fireside Chats *became a template example of a president using his personal charisma in broadcast media.*

My friends:

I want to talk for a few minutes with the people of the United States about banking – to talk with the comparatively few who understand the mechanics of banking, but more particularly with the overwhelming majority of you who use banks for the making of deposits and the drawing of checks.

I want to tell you what has been done in the last few days, and why it was done, and what the next steps are going to be. I recognize that the many proclamations from State capitols and from Washington, the legislation, the Treasury regulations, and so forth, couched for the most part in banking and legal terms, ought to be explained for the benefit of the average citizen. I owe this, in particular, because of the fortitude and the good temper with which everybody has accepted the inconvenience and hardships of the banking holiday. And I know that when you understand what we in Washington have been about, I shall continue to have your cooperation as fully as I have had your sympathy and your help during the past week.

First of all, let me state the simple fact that when you deposit money in a bank, the bank does not put the money into a safe deposit vault. It invests your money in many different forms of credit – in bonds, in commercial paper, in mortgages and in many other kinds of loans. In other words, the bank puts your money to work to keep the wheels of industry and of agriculture turning around. A comparatively small part of the money that you put into the bank is kept in currency – an amount which in normal times is wholly sufficient to cover the cash needs of the average citizen. In other words, the total amount of all the currency in the country is only a comparatively small proportion of the total deposits in all the banks of the country.

What, then, happened during the last few days of February and the first few days of March? Because of undermined confidence on the part of the public, there was a general rush by a large portion of our population to turn bank deposits into currency or gold – a rush so great that the soundest banks couldn't get enough currency to meet the demand. The reason for this was that on the spur of the moment it was, of course, impossible to sell perfectly sound assets of a bank and convert them into cash, except at panic prices far below their real value. By the afternoon of March third, a week ago last Friday, scarcely a bank in the country was open to do business. Proclamations closing them, in whole or in part, had been issued by the Governors in almost all the states. It was then that I issued the proclamation providing for the national bank holiday, and this was the first step in the Government's reconstruction of our financial and economic fabric.

The second step, last Thursday, was the legislation promptly and patriotically passed by the Congress confirming my proclamation and broadening my powers so that it became possible in view of the requirement of time to extend the holiday and lift the ban of that holiday gradually in the days to come. This law also gave authority to develop a program of rehabilitation of our banking facilities. And I want to tell our citizens in every part of the Nation that the national Congress – Republicans and Democrats alike – showed by this action a devotion to public welfare and a realization of the emergency and the necessity for speed that it is difficult to match in all our history.

The third stage has been the series of regulations permitting the banks to continue their functions to take care of the distribution of food and household necessities and the payment of payrolls.

This bank holiday, while resulting in many cases in great inconvenience, is affording us the opportunity to supply the currency necessary to meet the situation. Remember that no sound bank is a dollar worse off than it was when it closed its doors last week. Neither is any bank which may turn out not to be in a position for immediate opening. The new law allows the twelve Federal Reserve Banks to issue additional currency on good assets and thus the banks that reopen will be able to meet every legitimate call. The new currency is being sent out by the Bureau of Engraving and Printing in large volume to every part of the country. It is sound currency because it is backed by actual, good assets.

Another question you will ask is this: Why are all the banks not to be reopened at the same time? The answer is simple and I know you will understand it: Your Government does not intend that the history of the past few years shall be repeated. We do not want and will not have another epidemic of bank failures.

As a result, we start tomorrow, Monday, with the opening of banks in the twelve Federal Reserve Bank cities – those banks, which on first examination by the Treasury, have already been found to be all right. That will be followed on Tuesday by the resumption of all other functions by banks already found to be sound in cities where there are recognized clearing houses. That means about two hundred and fifty cities of the United States. In other words, we are moving as fast as the mechanics of the situation will allow us.

"IF YOU CAN'T STAND THE HEAT ..."

Harry S. Truman

1884–1972
33rd President: April 12, 1945–January 20, 1953

Early in 1952, President Harry S. Truman announced that he would not be seeking another presidential term. This quotation appeared in Time *magazine (April 28, 1952). The system he refers to is the presidential approval powers, giving him both a heavy workload and heavy responsibilities. During his years in the White House, Truman had had to cope with the end of World War II, the bombing of Hiroshima and Nagasaki, the beginning of the Korean War, the financial hardships of post-war America, and the looming Cold War. As the sign on his desk in the Oval Office said, "The Buck Stops Here," and after seven years of struggling to get legislation past Congress, and now in his late 60s, he felt that he had done as much as he could.*

One of the many results of the system gives the President a good many hot potatoes to handle – but the President gets a lot of hot potatoes from every direction anyhow, and a man who can't handle them has no business in that job. That makes me think of a saying that I used to hear from my old friend and colleague on the Jackson

County Court. He said, "Harry, if you can't stand the heat, you better get out of the kitchen."

TELEVISION DEBATE WITH JIMMY CARTER

Gerald Ford

1913–2006
38th President: August 9, 1974–January 20, 1977

One of the most inescapable features of the presidency in modern times is the media focus. Anyone spending a period of four to eight years having their every public word dissected by millions of people is likely to make a few mistakes … or quite a few. This little gem was spoken by Gerald Ford during his 1976 election campaign.

There is no Soviet domination of Eastern Europe and there never will be any under a Ford administration.

SPEECH TO THE REPUBLICAN NATIONAL CONVENTION

George H. W. Bush

1924

41st President: January 20, 1989–January 20, 1993

At the Republican Convention on August 18, Vice President George H. W. Bush accepted his party's nomination as presidential candidate. His acceptance – often called the "thousand points of light" speech – lifted his poll rating. He detailed his opposition to abortion and his support for gun rights, the death penalty, and saying the Pledge of Allegiance in schools. He finished the speech with a pledge on taxes, which has become one of the defining soundbites of his political career, although it backfired on him in the 1992 elections: because he was not able to stop Congress raising taxes to reduce the budget deficit, the Clinton campaign used this to label Bush as untrustworthy.

And I'm the one who will not raise taxes. My opponent now says he'll raise them as a last resort, or a third resort. But when a politician talks like that, you know that's one resort he'll be checking into. My opponent, my opponent won't rule out raising taxes. But I will. And the Congress will push me to raise taxes and I'll say no. And they'll push, and I'll say no, and they'll push again, and I'll say, to them, "Read my lips: no new taxes."

STATEMENT ON HIS TESTIMONY BEFORE THE GRAND JURY

Bill Clinton

———•———

1946

42nd President: January 20, 1993–January 20, 2001

Persistent claims of inappropriate behavior – first with Paula Jones and then Monica Lewinsky – dogged President Bill Clinton through the first half of his second term, although he had consistently denied any wrong-doing. However, when evidence did emerge, he was forced to testify before the Grand Jury that he had lied in his precious sworn deposition. The independent counsel he mentions is Kenneth Starr, who had also spent years ferreting out details of the Clintons' business dealings over what came to be known as Whitewatergate. Although much of the detail that appeared in the press was manufactured or exaggerated, President Clinton's presidency was weakened and the nature of the scandals may have contributed to the Republican victory of November 2000.

This afternoon in this room, from this chair, I testified before the Office of Independent Counsel and the Grand Jury.

I answered their questions truthfully, including questions about my private life, questions no American citizen would ever want to answer.

Still, I must take complete responsibility for all my actions, both public and private. And that is why I am speaking to you tonight.

As you know, in a deposition in January, I was asked questions about my relationship with Monica Lewinsky. While my answers were legally accurate, I did not volunteer information.

Indeed, I did have a relationship with Ms Lewinsky that was not appropriate. In fact, it was wrong. It constituted a critical lapse in judgment and a personal failure on my part for which I am solely and completely responsible.

But I told the Grand Jury today and I say to you now that at no time did I ask anyone to lie, to hide or destroy evidence or to take any other unlawful action.

I know that my public comments and my silence about this matter gave a false impression. I misled people, including even my wife. I deeply regret that.

I can only tell you I was motivated by many factors. First, by a desire to protect myself from the embarrassment of my own conduct.

I was also very concerned about protecting my family. The fact that these questions were being asked in a politically inspired lawsuit, which has since been dismissed, was a consideration, too.

In addition, I had real and serious concerns about an independent counsel investigation that began with private business dealings 20 years ago; dealings, I might add, about which an independent federal agency found no evidence of any wrongdoing by me or my wife over two years ago.

The independent counsel investigation moved on to my staff and friends, then into my private life. And now the investigation itself is under investigation.

This has gone on too long, cost too much and hurt too many innocent people.

Now, this matter is between me, the two people I love most – my wife and our daughter – and our God. I must put it right, and I am prepared to do whatever it takes to do so.

Nothing is more important to me personally. But it is private, and I intend to reclaim my family life for my family. It's nobody's business but ours.

Even presidents have private lives. It is time to stop the pursuit of personal destruction and the prying into private lives and get on with our national life.

Our country has been distracted by this matter for too long, and I take my responsibility for my part in all of this. That is all I can do.

Now it is time – in fact, it is past time – to move on.

We have important work to do – real opportunities to seize, real problems to solve, real security matters to face.

And so tonight, I ask you to turn away from the spectacle of the past seven months, to repair the fabric of our national discourse, and to return our attention to all the challenges and all the promise of the next American century.

Thank you for watching. And good night.

SPEECH ON THE KYOTO PROTOCOLS

George W. Bush

1946
43rd President: January 20, 2001–January 20, 2009

On June 11, 2001, President George W. Bush stood in the Rose Garden of the White House to explain his reasons for not ratifying the 1997 Kyoto Protocol on Climate Change. First, he felt that it would impact unfairly on U.S. industries and therefore the U.S. economy, particularly in relation to China – which had no limits imposed. Second, a recent report he had seen raised questions about the validity of the science that linked the increased amounts of man-made gases in the atmosphere with climate change. The protocol did not come into force until 2005, after the Russian Government ratified it, taking the number of ratifying countries above the required limit.

Good morning. I've just met with senior members of my administration who are working to develop an effective and science-based approach to addressing the important issues of global climate change [...]

The issue of climate change respects no border. Its effects cannot be reined in by an army nor advanced by any ideology. Climate change, with its potential to impact every corner of the world, is an issue that must be addressed by the world.

The Kyoto Protocol was fatally flawed in fundamental ways. But the process used to bring nations together to discuss our joint response to climate change is an important one.

That is why I am today committing the United States of America to work within the United Nations framework and elsewhere to develop with our friends and allies and nations throughout the world an effective and science-based response to the issue of global warming [...]

First, we know the surface temperature of the earth is warming. It has risen by .6 degrees Celsius over the past 100 years. There was a warming trend from the 1890s to the 1940s. Cooling from the 1940s to the 1970s. And then sharply rising temperatures from the 1970s to today.

There is a natural greenhouse effect that contributes to warming. Greenhouse gases trap heat, and thus warm the earth because they prevent a significant proportion of infrared radiation from escaping into space. Concentration of greenhouse gases, especially CO_2, have increased substantially since the beginning of the industrial revolution. And the National Academy of Sciences indicate that the increase is due in large part to human activity.

Yet, the Academy's report tells us that we do not know how much effect natural fluctuations in climate may have had on warming. We do not know how much our climate could, or will change in the future. We do not know how fast change will occur, or even how some of our actions could impact it [...]

Our country, the United States, is the world's largest emitter of manmade greenhouse gases. We account for almost 20 percent of the world's manmade greenhouse emissions. We also account for about one-quarter of the world's economic output. We recognize the responsibility to reduce our emissions. We also recognize the other part of the story – that the rest of the world emits 80 percent of all greenhouse gases. And many of those emissions come from developing countries.

This is a challenge that requires a 100 percent effort; ours, and the rest of the world's. The world's second-largest emitter of greenhouse gases is China. Yet, China was entirely exempted from the requirements of the Kyoto Protocol.

India and Germany are among the top emitters. Yet, India was also exempt from Kyoto. These and other developing countries that are experiencing rapid growth face challenges in reducing their emissions without harming their economies. We want to work cooperatively with these countries in their efforts to reduce greenhouse emissions and maintain economic growth.

Kyoto also failed to address two major pollutants that have an impact on warming: black soot and tropospheric ozone. Both are proven health hazards. Reducing both would not only address climate change, but also dramatically improve people's health.

Kyoto is, in many ways, unrealistic. Many countries cannot meet their Kyoto targets. The targets themselves were arbitrary and not based upon science. For America, complying with those mandates would have a negative economic impact, with layoffs of workers and price increases for consumers. And when you evaluate all these flaws, most reasonable people will understand that it's not sound public policy [...]

The UN Framework Convention on Climate Change commences to stabilizing concentrations at a level that will prevent dangerous human interference with the climate; but no one knows what that level is. The United States has spent $18 billion on climate research since 1990 – three times as much as any other country, and more than Japan and all 15 nations of the EU combined.

Today, I make our investment in science even greater. My administration will establish the U.S. Climate Change Research Initiative to study areas of uncertainty and identify priority areas where investments can make a difference. I'm directing my Secretary of Commerce, working with other agencies, to set priorities for additional investments in climate change research, review such investments, and to improve coordination amongst federal agencies. We will fully fund high-priority areas for climate change science over the next five years. We'll also provide resources to build climate observation systems in developing countries and encourage other developed nations to match our American commitment [...]

So we're creating the National Climate Change Technology Initiative to strengthen research at universities and national labs, to enhance partnerships in applied research, to develop improved technology for measuring and monitoring gross and net greenhouse gas emissions, and to fund demonstration projects for cutting-edge technologies, such as bioreactors and fuel cells.

Even with the best science, even with the best technology, we all know the United States cannot solve this global problem alone. We're building partnerships within the Western Hemisphere and with other like-minded countries. Last week, Secretary Powell signed a new CONCAUSA Declaration with the countries of Central America, calling for cooperative efforts on science research, monitoring and measuring of emissions, technology development, and investment in forest conservation.

We will work with the Inter-American Institute for Global Change Research and other institutions to better understand regional impacts of climate change. We will establish a partnership to monitor and mitigate emissions. And at home, I call on Congress to work with my administration on the initiatives to enhance conservation and energy efficiency outlined in my energy plan, to implement the increased use of renewables, natural gas and hydropower that are outlined in the plan, and to increase the generation of safe and clean nuclear power [...]

Our approach must be flexible to adjust to new information and take advantage of new technology. We must always act to ensure continued economic growth and prosperity for our citizens and for citizens throughout the world. We should pursue market-based incentives and spur technological innovation.

And, finally, our approach must be based on global participation, including that of developing countries whose net greenhouse gas emissions now exceed those in the developed countries.

Our administration will be creative. We're committed to protecting our environment and improving our economy, to acting at home and working in concert with the world. This is an administration that will make commitments we can keep, and keep the commitments that we make.

I look forward to continued discussions with our friends and allies about this important issue.

INDEX